THE CAMBRIDGE CONNECTION

THE CAMBRIDGE CONNECTION
AND THE ELIZABETHAN SETTLE-
MENT OF 1559

Winthrop S. Hudson

Duke University Press *Durham, North Carolina* 1980

© 1980, Duke University Press
L.C.C. card no. 79–56513
I.S.B.N. 0–8223–0440–6
Printed in the United States of
America by Heritage Printers

Library of Congress Cataloging in Publication Data
Hudson, Winthrop Still, 1911–
    The Cambridge connection and the Elizabethan
settlement of 1559.
    Includes index.
    1. Great Britain—History—Elizabeth, 1558–1603.
2. Elizabeth, Queen of England, 1533–1603. I. Title.
DA355.H85   942.05'5   79–56513
ISBN 0–8223–0440–6

To Katherine Hudson Rogers

For she is wise, if I can judge of her,
And fair she is, if that mine eyes be true,
And true she is, as she hath prov'd herself.

The Merchant of Venice, II, vi

CONTENTS

ACKNOWLEDGMENTS

Expression of appreciation to those who have provided aid and encouragement in the writing of a book is always a pleasure. It calls to mind memories of friends, colleagues, and institutions that have helped along the way. The "Cambridge connection" has lurked half-suppressed at the edge of my consciousness since the beginning of my academic career when W. K. Jordan induced me to give serious attention to one of the members of the Cambridge "Athenian tribe." It was not until 1975, however, when the National Endowment for the Humanities awarded me a Senior Fellowship and the Folger Shakespeare Library provided a grant-in-aid, that I was able to give undivided attention to exploring the network of relationships existing among those who helped fashion the Elizabethan settlement of 1559. This was pure bounty after a long period during which my scholarly pursuits were programmed in part by the enticements of publishers. I feel equal appreciation for opportunities for continuing research, reflection, and writing provided by the several institutions with which I have been affiliated: the theological school with the cumbersome name of Colgate Rochester Divinity School/Bexley Hall/Crozer Theological Seminary, the University of Rochester, and the University of North Carolina.

As every author confesses, the errors of fact and interpretation are my own, and they would have been more numerous had it not been for the frank criticisms of many who have been kind enough to discuss with me my ideas and to read, in whole or in part, drafts of my manuscript. At several key points, readers have strengthened my argument. Elsewhere they have contributed new insights to an extent that I am hesitant to claim credit for what I have written.

I am especially grateful to G. R. Elton for his gracious hospitality, advice, and encouragement during a period of residence and research at Cambridge. I am indebted to him for detailed comments which have kept me from a number of egregious blunders. I was equally fortunate that Paul Needham of the Pierpont Morgan Library was willing to give freely of his time and to place at my disposal his unrivaled knowledge of the Edwardian court and of affairs at Cambridge as they related to John Cheke and his friends. Wallace MacCaffrey has been kind and has helped me even more than he may suspect. This is also true of Paul Seaver who identified key issues with which I had to come to terms when I presented a synopsis of my initial conclusions at a session of the American Society of Church History. Perez Zagorin has been equally gracious with his suggestions and encouragement. Wyndham M. Southgate responded far beyond any claim of friendship when he subjected the completed manuscript to critical examination, giving detailed attention to both substance and style. Others who have been helpful in a variety of ways include C. W. Dugmore, H. Shelton Smith, Peter Kaufman, Thomas Rumsey, Grant Wacker, and my wife, who has a ready eye for infelicities of expression. F. W. Hasler of the History of Parliament Trust with characteristic kindness sat by my side as we went through the biographical files compiled by the Trust.

To forestall any puzzlement, I should acknowledge that I have not made use of Norman Jones' analysis, in his Cambridge University dissertation, of the way in which the House of Lords complicated the task of reaching a religious settlement. This has been a deliberate choice for I understand that he has plans for publication and I have not wished to disclose prematurely his conclusions. His research, I have been informed, indicates that intransigence in the upper chamber was the chief problem confronting Elizabeth and her advisors in effecting a religious settlement. As W. P. Haugaard made clear, the recalcitrance of the Lords was aided and abetted by members of the unreformed and unaltered Marian Convocation.

As one looks back one would not wish to forget the courtesy of librarians and archivists both in England and the United States. The graciousness of Ashbel G. Brice of the Duke University Press has been unfailing and is remembered with appreciation, as is the perceptive and discriminating edition of the manuscript by Joanne Ferguson.

WINTHROP S. HUDSON

Chapel Hill, N.C.

THE CAMBRIDGE CONNECTION

I. INTRODUCTION

Books often evolve, having a life cycle of their own. This account of "the Cambridge connection" is the by-product of an earlier interest in John Ponet, Edwardian bishop of Rochester and then of Winchester, who died in exile after writing a minor classic in the history of political thought (*A Shorte Treatise of Politike Power, and of the True Obedience which Subjectes Owe to Kynges and Other Civile Governours*, 1556).

Ponet belonged to a group of brilliant young scholars at Cambridge which began to coalesce about 1535 around a common interest in promoting the Erasmian pronunciation of Greek, a reform that was to be vigorously and vehemently opposed by Stephen Gardiner after he became chancellor of the university. The brightest light and leading spirit of this "Athenian tribe" was John Cheke, later to become tutor to young Prince Edward. Two other members were Thomas Smith, known to posterity as the author of *De republica Anglorum*, and Roger Ascham, famed as the author of *The Schoolmaster*.

The first aspect of the activity of these young men which I found interesting was their success in winning a widening circle of support in the university. This was especially true of John Cheke whose eager enthusiasm was contagious and was reinforced by a winsomeness of spirit which captured the admiration and affection of many members of the university. Thus the bond of a common interest was strengthened by ties of friendship, and the intimacy of their relationship to one another led to further joint concerns. Within little more than a decade, these Athenians had become numerous enough and influential enough to dominate the university, obtaining a near monopoly of such university posts as vice-chancellor, public orator, and the regius professorships, as well as the masterships of most of the colleges.

A second intriguing feature of this group of youthful scholars, linked by friendship, common interests, and mutual concerns, was the migration of a considerable number of them from Cambridge

3

to London. Some, including Cheke, William Grindal, Roger Ascham, John Aylmer, James Haddon, and Thomas Wilson, were summoned to court to serve as tutors and chaplains to members of the royal family and in the households of some of the nobility. Others, including William Cecil, Walter Mildmay, and Nicholas Bacon, came to London to study at the Inns of Court and to serve in subordinate capacities as "literate" clerks. Still others were sent abroad to gain experience in foreign service. Both those who served as clerks and those who were sent abroad were well placed to learn the skills of statecraft and to expand their circle of friends, while those who served as tutors were in a strategic position to shape the minds and gain the confidence of children of future importance and influence. Meanwhile, the bonds of friendship and common interests were being tightened, mostly through marriage, by an interlacing network of family relationships.

Equally intriguing, as the study progressed, was the relationship of these Cambridge Athenians (and of the friends they subsequently acquired) to the Elizabethan settlement of 1559. It was not surprising to find that they provided Elizabeth with a university-trained pool of potential "civil servants" and "ecclesiastics" from which to draw personnel to staff her regime. What was surprising was the extent to which Elizabeth utilized members of this relatively close-knit circle of friends for top positions in both government and church.

The pursuit of this Cambridge connection from 1535 to 1560 led to an unanticipated discovery of some consequence. The discovery was the fresh light shed on the Elizabethan settlement of 1559 when approached from the perspective of those who participated in it. When one begins with a later period and then moves backward in time, a quite different picture is presented from that which emerges when the settlement is viewed from the perspective provided by moving forward to 1559 from the earlier years. Instead of bringing to it preconceptions derived from later developments, one is freed to examine the evidence in terms of what the participants themselves believed they were doing.

Hindsight can be misleading. It can lead one to assume, for example, that the tension between the queen and the Commons which was so conspicuous a feature of later Parliaments must have been present in 1559. Reading the record in the light of the existing

Cambridge connection, on the other hand, suggests that there was more consensus than conflict between the queen, the council, the Commons, and the chosen leaders of her reconstituted church than has commonly been supposed. It also suggests that the common outlook held firm for several months after the 1559 Parliament was dissolved. There were moments of anxiety, to be sure, for the strategy being directed by Cecil and pursued by the queen was not made clear even to the participants. Even though reassurances were given, tactical shifts created further moments of confusion and dismay. When the break came between the queen and the clergy who helped fashion and staff the religious settlement, it was quite inadvertent and unanticipated. It did not occur until late in 1559 and it was papered over temporarily in 1560.

It is puzzling that the existence and importance of this Cambridge connection has been overlooked for so long. Perhaps it has been because few have ever thought of Cecil as a Greek scholar and no one has given much thought to the time Elizabeth spent reading Greek with Roger Ascham or of attempts she had made to test her skill in making Greek translations. More realistic are two other explanations. Many historians have been preoccupied with attempts to identify "factions" representing differing points of view at the time of Elizabeth's accession. Other historians, pursuing a similar line of inquiry, have sought to find some partisan significance attached to persons who went into exile under Mary. The assumption was that the exile must have provided a line of demarcation for group identity. Actually it did not. The exiles were a divided, not a unified group.

The Marian exile was particularly misleading for it seemed to provide such an obvious line of division. While some members of what is called the Cambridge connection did go into exile, others did not. Some simply withdrew from public life, some were able to make an accommodation which enabled them to function in minor official capacities during Mary's reign, some were not put to the test, and some went into hiding or made themselves as inconspicuous as possible. The response to the Marian regime varied according to differences in temperament, in the intensity and character of religious convictions, and in the individual's perception of the danger of arrest.

The Marian exile, therefore, has served to obscure the relationships which continued to exist among those who constituted this informal circle of friends. Ties were maintained between those who went into exile, such as Richard Cox, Edmund Grindal, Edwin Sandys, Anthony Cooke, and Francis Knollys, and those who did not, such as Matthew Parker, William Bill, Nicholas Bacon, and William Cecil. By obscuring connections which had no relationship to the exile, preoccupation with the Marian exile as a line of demarcation has made it difficult to perceive the community of interest and intimacy of friendship which did unite those who were brought into Elizabeth's service at the beginning of her reign.

It should not be supposed that these friends who helped fashion and staff the religious settlement of 1559 came together at the accession of Elizabeth with any carefully articulated preexisting consensus as to an optimal settlement, to say nothing of an agreed upon strategy or policy for achieving it. There was no great difference of opinion among them, however, for they shared a common outlook and a common background. Moreover, they were ready to work together as friends in a relationship of mutual trust. A clue to the type of thinking they represented is provided by those who did go into exile. Strassburg was their chief headquarters, and from Strassburg they intervened in "the troubles at Frankfort" to defend the use of the 1552 Edwardian prayer book. But, as subsequent events made clear, they were not wedded to the retention of much of the "scenic apparatus" traditionally associated with divine worship. Indeed, they were offended by many of these "fooleries."

To the extent that there was a strategy in 1559, and few would question that there was one, it was a strategy worked out by William Cecil and the queen and it was subject to tactical modification as changing circumstances warranted. Members of the circle of friends identified as the Cambridge connection were consulted and used at almost every step to help forward the settlement, but more often than not they were left very much in the dark with regard to the tactical moves that were being taken, and they were not always certain what these tactical moves portended. In spite of reassurances, not being taken completely into confidence caused them anxious moments. Cecil and Elizabeth, on the other hand, were both accustomed to and often found it necessary to keep their own counsel when dealing with the practical exigencies of delicate political maneuvers.

The reader may find repeated reminders of some relationships among those grouped together under the rubric of the Cambridge connection occasionally monotonous and perhaps unnecessary. Such ties of university days, subsequent friendship, and sometimes of family, however, are not incidental. They served as the matrix which facilitated the development of a common attitude of mind, outlook, and mutual trust during two and a half decades preceding the accession of Elizabeth. The reader also may wish to note the way in which a smaller group of friends—William Butts, Thomas Cranmer, and Anthony Denny—at an earlier time worked together. Their informal mode of getting things done was to be prophetic of the future. Butts was physician to Henry VIII and was the primary link between the young Athenians at Cambridge and the court. In the same fashion, the reader may wish to give attention to how John Jewel, an Oxford scholar, was drawn into the Athenian orbit and became part of the Cambridge connection. Finally, the reader should be alerted to an important subordinate theme represented by scattered indications of William Cecil's brother-father relationship to many women who, in time of need for help and understanding, turned to him as one who could be trusted.

In addition to calling attention to the coalescing in the last years of Henry VIII of what has been called the Cambridge connection, tracing its further development under Edward VI, and indicating at some length how the existence of this circle of friends helps clarify ambiguities of the Elizabethan settlement, this study also contributes to historical understanding at two other points. First, attention is drawn to an early phase of the development of an incipient "civil service" that was able to provide a degree of continuity, stability, and "professionalism" at court. Second, the study illustrates an initial stage of the transition from an earlier to a more modern structure of social and political relationships. More specifically it should serve to document a growing displacement in importance of the vertical relationships of loyalty, trust, and obligation so characteristic of feudal society by the increasingly dominant horizontal relationships of post-feudal society.

Although this study suggests new perspectives to an understanding of the years between 1535 and the accession of Elizabeth and a quite radically new analysis of the settlement of 1559, in the field of scholarship it can best be regarded as an extended footnote of considerable significance to the initial chapters of two studies of broader scope and major importance—Wallace MacCaffrey's *The Shaping of the Elizabethan Regime* (Princeton, 1968) and Patrick Collinson's *The Elizabethan Puritan Movement* (Berkeley, 1967). While it does bring into question prevailing understandings of what occurred during the first year of Elizabeth's reign, it in no way qualifies MacCaffrey's and Collinson's incisive and perceptive analyses of the course of events in subsequent years. Indeed, it serves to strengthen their respective arguments.

II. WILLIAM CECIL AND THE FORMA-TION OF THE ELIZABETHAN GOVERN-MENT

The accession of Elizabeth to the English throne on November 17, 1558, was followed by a burst of intense activity, bringing to an end a period of drift which had left the country in a precarious situation. The treasury was depleted. Credit was overextended. The coinage was debased. War with France was a drain on revenues and a source of instability. The relationship with Spain was uncertain. Conditions in Scotland demanded a decisive English response. Equally urgent were divisive religious issues which desperately needed to be resolved. Within scarcely more than a year all these problems had been faced. Personnel had been recruited and actions taken which were to give the Elizabethan regime its lasting shape and character.

By a stroke of fate the government had been placed in capable hands. Mary's death had been anticipated, and with startling suddenness there were plans for everything. As a result, the immediate transition from the preceding reign was effected without undue strain and tension. Even bishops firmly wedded to Rome were remarkably passive and cooperated at points where their religious loyalties were not specifically put to a test. This striking accomplishment within a relatively brief span of time is one reason scholars have found the initial months of Elizabeth's reign so fascinating to analyze, assess, and interpret.

ELIZABETH AND CECIL

At the center of the planning which preceded Elizabeth's accession, and the burst of activity which followed, was William Cecil, Elizabeth's longtime friend and confidant. The new queen initiated her government on Sunday, November 20, 1558, with two statements of policy. She spoke first before all who had assembled at Hatfield House, announcing her intention to keep the membership of the Privy Council relatively small in number.

9

I desire you all, my lords, chiefly you of the nobility, every-one in his degree and power, to be assistant to me. . . . My purpose is to require of you all nothing more but faithful hearts in such service as from time to time shall be in your powers towards the preservation of me and this common-wealth. . . .

And for counsel and advice, I shall accept you of my nobility and such others of you . . . [as] in consultation I shall think meet and shortly appoint. . . . Also I will join to their aid and for ease of their burden [in administration] others meet for my service.

And they which I shall not appoint, let them not think the same for any disability in them, but for that I consider a multi-tude doth make rather discord and confusion than good coun-sel.

With these words Elizabeth indicated a sharp break with the prac-tice of attempting to work with a large council which too often had proved to be unwieldy, inefficient, and torn by factionalism. She indicated also an intention of separating at some points, for "ease" of "burden," policy-making and administrative responsibilities.

Following this plea for support and brief explanation of the policy she planned to pursue, Elizabeth dismissed most of those who had gathered at Hatfield to proffer their fealty. Eight or nine were asked to remain for what was in effect the first meeting of Elizabeth's new council.[1] To them she made clear the person upon whom she would chiefly rely for counsel and advice. As Cecil stepped forward to be sworn to the council, Elizabeth said to him:

I give you this charge that you shall be of my privy council and content to take pains for me and my realm. This judgment I have of you that you will not be corrupted by any manner of gift and that you will be faithful to the state; and that, without respect of my private will, you will give me that counsel which you think best; and if you know anything necessary to be

1. Ralph Sadler remained, not as a prospective councilor, but as an emis-sary from those of the old council who were looking after routine affairs in London. These were most likely Nicholas Heath, archbishop of York, who had been Mary's lord chancellor, and two long-time bureaucrats, John Mason and William Petre. At least these were the three who were authorized the next day to transact urgent business in the city.

declared to me of secrecy, you shall show it to myself only. And assure yourself I will not fail to keep taciturnity therein. And therefore herewith I charge you.

It was striking for Cecil to be singled out in this fashion. Elizabeth's charge was more than an expression of confidence, confirming the trust she long had placed in him and his judgment. It indicated that Cecil was to have a special relationship to her as the foremost of her councilors, that as her principal secretary he was to be her chief minister.

Cecil had not waited until his official appointment as principal secretary on November 20, 1558, to begin functioning in this capacity. On the day of Mary's death and Elizabeth's accession, November 17, he had moved with speed and confidence to assume control of the government. He had drafted memoranda, first of things to be done, and then of matters to be done immediately, and he proceeded to see that the items listed were handled with dispatch, enlisting Nicholas Throckmorton as his chief aide. While Cecil was putting finishing touches on the proclamation declaring Elizabeth to be queen as "the only right heir by blood and lawful succession," Throckmorton was taking the black enamelled ring, removed from Mary's hand, to Elizabeth at Hatfield as evidence that Mary's death was no mere rumor. Following the joint session of Parliament at nine o'clock in the morning when Elizabeth was acknowledged to be queen, several of the lords, accompanied by heralds, were sent to key points in the city publicly to proclaim her accession. Within hours the proclamation had been printed and posted to the sheriffs in the shires, that her accession might similarly be proclaimed throughout the realm. On the same day, guards were changed at the Tower, ports closed, border garrisons alerted. A final item listed as requiring immediate attention was to give careful consideration to selecting the preacher for Paul's Cross that "no occasion be given by him to stir any dispute touching the governance of the realm."[2]

2. Paul's Cross, an open-air pulpit in the cathedral yard, was more than a preaching station. It was a place where official proclamations were read, where the government could make known its mind. It was a place for propaganda, more a stage than a pulpit, where the preacher had opportunity to influence a large cross section of the populace. See Millar Maclure, *The Paul's Cross Sermons* (Toronto, 1958). A letter from Grindal to Cecil, October 28, 1562, indicates the nature of the preacher's role and the serious-

By nightfall Cecil's friend from Cambridge days, William Bill, had been secured to preach at the Cross on the following Sunday, November 20, the day when Elizabeth was meeting with her Privy Council for the first time at Hatfield. Bill was instructed to use the opportunity to bid the people gathered at the Cross to be quiet and orderly.3

There are several indications that Cecil had been at work as Elizabeth's chief agent prior to Mary's death. Mary was taken ill on August 17, 1558, and it soon was apparent that she had not long to live. Early in November the council had persuaded Mary to name Elizabeth her successor, and Cecil must have been deeply involved in Elizabeth's affairs a few days later. On November 10, when the Spanish ambassador found Mary dying, he hastened to see Elizabeth. He reported to Philip of Spain the impressions he gained from the interview, mentioning the names of those he believed would be members of her council. And then he added: "I am told for certain that Cecil, who was secretary to King Edward, will be her secretary also. He is said to be a prudent and virtuous man, albeit a heretic."4 The ambassador's report is important in two respects. It shows that at least a week before Mary's death Elizabeth was making plans for her succession, and it notes as the only definite information the ambassador had secured, the fact that Cecil was to be her secretary. The key relationship of Cecil to Elizabeth seems to have been no secret. Three or four days before Mary's death, Nicholas Heath initiated a conversation with Cecil about the office of lord chancellor. Heath was not well and expressed a desire to be relieved of the post. Although Cecil solicited Heath's opinion about possible

---

ness with which he approached it. "I pray you let me understand whether it may be certainly avouched that the king of Navarre, the second Julian, is killed. I intend (God willing) to preach at the Cross next Sunday, and upon occasion offered would peradventure make some mention of God's judgment over him, if the same be true, else not. If there be any other matter which ye wish to be uttered there for the present state, I would be pleased to know it in time if your leisure will serve." *Remains of Archbishop Grindal* (Cambridge, 1863), p. 253.

3. Having been deprived under Mary, Bill was reinstated as master of Trinity College, as well as being made almoner to the queen, elected provost of Eton, and appointed dean of Westminster.

4. Patrick F. Tytler, ed., *England under the Reigns of Edward VI and Mary* (London, 1839), II, 498–99. See also Conyers Read, *Mr. Secretary Cecil and Queen Elizabeth* (London, 1955), p. 118.

replacements, Heath gained the impression that Elizabeth wished him to retain the chancellorship.[5] Further evidence that Cecil's close relationship to the prospective queen was taken for granted is provided by Throckmorton's memoranda of advice to Elizabeth, the first portion of which was drafted prior to Mary's death. Throckmorton simply assumed that Cecil was to have a key role. He felt it to be urgent, however, that Cecil should be called "to exercise the room of secretary about your person forthwith."[6]

Throckmorton's sense of urgency and emphasis on "forthwith" was undoubtedly related to Elizabeth's need for and dependence upon someone skilled and trustworthy in affairs of state. She was young, inexperienced, had no training in statecraft, and for extended periods of time had been excluded and isolated from the court. While she had been an apt pupil in learning the lessons necessary for personal survival, the intricacies of monetary, fiscal, and foreign policy, to say nothing of the details of legal and administrative procedures, were matters which she could only have observed from a distance. Moreover, she had neither the background nor the knowledge to evaluate the specialized competencies of persons she would need to recruit for her government. Elizabeth was beginning as a novice who quickly displayed her own mettle, and, whether or not she needed Throckmorton's urging to appoint Cecil forthwith, this is what she did, making it clear at the time that he was to be the councilor upon whom she would chiefly rely.

The partnership of Cecil and Elizabeth, which was to last until his death in 1598, had long antecedents. Cecil had been about the court and in and out of her chambers when his friends, first William Grindal and then more briefly, Roger Ascham, had been her tutors. It has been suggested that occasionally Cecil participated in the instruction of both Edward and Elizabeth. In addition to being close to those who were officially charged with providing instruction, Cecil enjoyed the friendship of Catherine Parr, who had sponsored what was referred to as the "royal nursery." Moreover, Cecil introduced his kinsman Thomas Parry to court and presumably was responsible for Parry's appointment in 1548 as Elizabeth's cofferer or steward. Even before 1550 when Elizabeth appointed Cecil as

5. Read, *Mr. Secretary Cecil*, pp. 122, 479n.
6. J. E. Neale, ed., "Sir Nicholas Throckmorton's Advice to Queen Elizabeth," *English Historical Review*, LXV (1950): 94.

"surveyor" or overseer of her estates and thus technically Parry's superior and supervisor, Parry was accustomed to consult Cecil with regard to the management of Elizabeth's properties. This is made evident by two letters from Parry to Cecil in 1549 discussing Elizabeth's business affairs. During Mary's reign Cecil continued to serve as Elizabeth's surveyor. The fees he received for this service are entered in his account books, but on one occasion he seems to have intimated that it would be better, i.e., safer, for Elizabeth if he did not see her.[7]

More revealing than these outward points of contact are Elizabeth's own indications of a highly personal regard for Cecil. On August 2, 1548, when Elizabeth was 14, a note appended to a letter from her governess, Catherine Ashley, was addressed "Unto thee my very friend, Master Cecil" and was signed "your friend Elizabeth." A year later, Elizabeth dictated a note to be added to a letter Thomas Parry was writing for her because of a "weakness" (injury) of her hand. "Write . . . to Mr. Cecil that I am well assured, though I send not daily to him, that he does not for all that daily forget me."[8] This latter note of assurance may have been related to the embarrassing and difficult situation in which Elizabeth found herself late in 1548 in connection with the Thomas Seymour "affair."

It is usually suggested that Cecil commanded Elizabeth's confidence because of his honesty, integrity, and loyalty, because of his reputation of not being bribable, because he never aspired to play the role of a courtier. It is true that Cecil did inspire trust and confidence in many people because of these qualities. One illustration is John Mason's comment when a rumor reached him at Brussels in 1554 that Cecil might succeed William Petre as secretary in Mary's council. Mason responded that he could not think of "so sufficient a successor," one "whose match . . . I know not within the realm of England."[9] And Cecil's capacity to inspire the trust and confidence

7. Read, *Mr. Secretary Cecil*, pp. 63–65, 116, 479n. Tytler, *England under the Reigns of Edward VI and Mary*, I, 202, 323, 425–26. Cecil had arranged with Elizabeth that he would have a deputy take care of most of the details associated with his position as her surveyor.

8. Mary A. E. Wood (Green), *Letters of Royal and Illustrious Ladies* (London, 1846), III, 221. Tytler, *England under the Reigns of Edward VI and Mary*, I, 425–26. Tytler may have misdated the letter, see Read, *Mr. Secretary Cecil*, p. 64.

9. F. G. Emmison, *Tudor Secretary, Sir William Petre at Court and Home* (London, 1961), p. 182.

of women was especially notable. Again, there are many examples. Elizabeth Gregory, lady Cromwell, is one. In 1552 she wrote Cecil: "Your great gentleness, many ways showed toward me, emboldeneth me to trouble you with these my letters." [10] The most vivid illustration of the confidence Cecil evoked is provided by the doughty Catherine Willoughby, duchess of Suffolk, when she heard of Cecil's appointment as principal secretary in September 1550. She wrote him: "I am content to become your partner . . . and I will abide all adventures in your ship, be the weather fair or foul." [11] The pledge of loyalty was later to be qualified, but the force of her initial spontaneous comment was not diminished by the fact that some years later she found herself in disagreement with Cecil and felt compelled to remind him of what she thought was his duty. Perhaps a major reason for the trust Cecil inspired among women was that he respected intelligent women at a time when there were numerous intelligent, highly-educated women at court and elsewhere among the wives and daughters of the nobility and the wealthier gentry. Cecil, for example, did not hesitate to solicit the aid of Catherine Willoughby, duchess of Suffolk, in affairs at court. He urged her on one occasion to return to court to help heal the breach between Seymour and Dudley.

Still Elizabeth's confidence in and devotion to Cecil seems to have been more deeply rooted, more emotionally based, than most similar relationships. It probably is to be explained in terms of her lonely childhood and adolescence. Hers was a childhood that taught her many things—patience, tenacity, courage, calculation, the will and determination to survive, a capacity for dissimulation, and an ability to keep her own counsel. But these are difficult lessons for a young girl to learn, and those who sustained her with help, friendship, or affection in her times of trouble were persons she did not forget in later years.

A forlorn child, buffeted from place to place, neglected by her father, Elizabeth found warmth and affection for the first time when Catherine Parr, Henry VIII's last wife, reassembled the children—Mary, Elizabeth, and Edward—at court and gave them motherly attention. What this meant to Elizabeth can be gleaned from a letter she wrote to Catherine, after having been removed from the

10. Wood (Green), *Letters of Royal and Illustrious Ladies*, III, 261.
11. Tytler, *England under the Reigns of Edward VI and Mary*, I, 323.

household, asking her to intercede with her father to permit her to return. She told the queen that the hope of being with her once again very soon was all that made her present situation tolerable. "In this my exile," she concluded, "I well know . . . your highness has had . . . much care and solicitude" for me, and I know you "have not forgotten me." The lonely child signed the letter your "most obedient daughter and faithful servant." [12]

Almost equally enlightening is a letter of Elizabeth to her half-sister Mary in 1547 which was prompted by the marriage of Catherine Parr to Thomas Seymour, the lord admiral, being solemnized in undignified haste and secrecy so soon after the death of the king.

> I cannot express to you . . . how much affliction I suffered when I was first informed of this marriage. . . . Neither you nor I, dearest sister, are in such a condition as to offer any obstacle thereto without running heavy risk of making our own lot much worse than it is. . . . I think then that the best course we can take is that of dissimulation, that the mortification may fall upon those who commit the fault. Let us console ourselves by making the best of what we cannot remedy. If our silence do us no honor, at least it will not draw down upon us such disasters as our own lamentation might induce. . . .
>
> With regard to the returning of visits, I do not see that you, who are the elder, are obliged to do this. But the position in which I stand obliges me to take other measures, the queen having shown me so great affection and done me so many kind offices that I must use tact . . . , for fear of appearing ungrateful. . . . However, I shall always pay much deference to your instructions and demands. [13]

Elizabeth's letter reveals, for one so young, unusual tact and canniness by exhibiting sympathetic regard for the the feelings of her sister while, at the same time, leaving herself sufficient room to pursue her own course. It also discloses Elizabeth's deep affection

12. *The Letters of Queen Elizabeth I*, ed. G. B. Harrison (London, 1968), p. 5. On other occasions, Elizabeth's letters to Catherine were signed "your humble daughter."
13. Wood (Green), *Letters of Royal and Illustrious Ladies*, III, 193–94.

for Catherine, while giving no hint that the budding adolescent of fourteen was in any way emotionally involved with Thomas Seymour, Catherine's new husband.

Elizabeth remained a member of Catherine's household after her letter to Mary. She engaged in happy "frolics," as they were later described, with Catherine and Thomas, often in Elizabeth's bed chamber. When Seymour began to indulge in this intimate playfulness without Catherine being present, such unseemly behavior gave rise to spreading gossip. To avoid scandal, Elizabeth and her attendants were packed off to live with the Anthony Dennys in Hertfordshire. Shortly thereafter, in September 1548, Catherine died. Thomas Seymour then, with schemes afoot which in January were to result in his arrest for treason, began to devise plans to marry Elizabeth, being aided and abetted in the project by Thomas Parry, Elizabeth's steward, and Catherine Ashley, her governess. This plan quickly became tied in with his other plots, and Elizabeth was placed in a most difficult and compromising situation. An investigation was made. Servants were questioned. People were hauled off to London for interrogation. Depositions were taken. And Elizabeth was subjected to intensive grilling. If ever a young girl needed a friend of experience to provide advice and counsel, to help her defend herself and avoid the pitfalls by which she might be betrayed into a seeming acquiescence in the lord admiral's intrigues, Elizabeth did.

The reason for sketching Elizabeth's dangerous plight when she was scarcely into her early teens is that Cecil is the person most likely to have come to her aid, thus solidifying a relationship of trust that was to endure for the next fifty years. There are several reasons to suspect that this was the case. First, Cecil already had established a firm friendship with Elizabeth. Second, he had a further tie to her through Thomas Parry. Third, as personal secretary and master of requests to Edward Seymour, the Protector Somerset, he was in a position to be of help. Fourth, he seems to have been ready on other occasions to help those in distress, and the Protector had previously given him delicate assignments to handle that required tact and diplomacy. Finally, it may be of some significance in confirming Cecil's role that all the correspondence, examinations, statements, depositions, confessions, and reports (51 items including a letter and confession of Elizabeth) relating to the "affair" were found systematically arranged among Cecil's papers at Hatfield House.[14] Other papers in the collection are either fugitive items or items having little relationship in time or substance to the Seymour affair. This suggests that the latter may have been a matter he had handled discreetly, taking the additional precaution of withdrawing the papers from the official files and retaining them in his own possession.

Whatever the reason for the close and intimate relationship of Cecil to Elizabeth, it is clear that Cecil was at center stage from the outset of her reign. By December 14, 1558, the Spanish ambassador was reporting that England is a "kingdom in the hands of young folks" and governed by "a young lass." He commented more specifically that the young queen's "comptroller [Parry] and her secretary Cecil govern the kingdom, and they tell me the earl of Bedford [Francis Russell] has a good deal to say." A few pages later he wrote that Cecil is "the man who does everything."[15]

THE PRIVY COUNCIL

Cecil may have been the key figure in Elizabeth's new government, but he was only one of a cluster of councilors and officials which gave the new regime its distinctive shape and character.

Appointments to the Privy Council proceeded slowly. The original nucleus of November 20, 1558, including both those at Hatfield and those in London, number 11 in all. Six of these were from Mary's council: the earls of Arundel (Henry Fitzalen) and Pembroke (William Herbert), the lord admiral (Edward Fiennes de Clinton), Nicholas Heath, John Mason, and William Petre. Six more from the old council also were to be retained, but several of these men either were old and soon died or were quietly dropped,[16] leaving a total of 8 who were to be retained as members of the council. The initial new members of November 20 were Ambrose Cave,

14. Samuel Haynes, ed., *A Collection of State Papers . . . Left by William Cecil, Lord Burghley, and Now Remaining at Hatfield House* (London, 1740), pp. 61–108.

15. *Calendar of State Papers, Spanish, 1558–67*, I, 7, 10.

16. Thomas Cheyney died before the year was out. William Paulet, marquis of Winchester, was in his eighties. Heath was not retained as lord chancellor and quietly dropped from the council. Mason, Petre, and Wotton were career bureaucrats, friends and former colleagues of Cecil, who had entered the service of the court under Henry VIII.

William Cecil, Thomas Parry, Edward Rogers, and Richard Sackville. The following day Francis Russell, earl of Bedford, appeared and was sworn to the council. On December 22 Nicholas Bacon, Cecil's brother-in-law, was admitted to the council, and on December 25 William Parr, having been restored as marquis of Northampton, became a member. Finally, on January 14, 1559, Francis Knollys, fresh from exile on the Continent, was sworn to the council. Thus by the time of Elizabeth's coronation, on the following day, the council included 9 new appointees, having been reduced from approximately 30 members under Mary to fewer than 20.

While the council was being formed, Cecil pushed forward on other fronts. On the day following Elizabeth's accession, Cecil called her attention to the crisis precipitated by the huge foreign debt that had been allowed to accumulate. The next day, even before the Privy Council met for the first time, Cecil brought Thomas Gresham to Hatfield to brief Elizabeth on the seriousness of the problem, and in December Gresham was dispatched to Antwerp to raise a loan to meet immediate needs and to remain there as "royal agent" to put England's foreign debts in order. This, in turn, was dependent upon financial reforms which William Paulet, marquis of Winchester, had already initiated as lord treasurer. A long-term bureaucrat, experienced and competent, Paulet was now a very old man. To assist him in carrying out the necessary financial reforms, the much younger Walter Mildmay, as gifted as Gresham in monetary management, was enlisted as chancellor of the exchequer, and Richard Sackville, former chancellor of the Court of Augmentations, was recruited to serve as undertreasurer. Walter Haddon, a distinguished "civil lawyer," was summoned on November 20, 1558, to appear before the council as a prelude to being appointed to serve jointly with Thomas Seckford, a "common lawyer" of considerable repute, as masters of the Court of Requests.

Other appointments were made with equal care. Nicholas Bacon, father of Francis Bacon, replaced Heath, the Marian lord chancellor, but with the title of lord keeper of the great seal. William Howard of Effingham was installed as chamberlain and Edward Rogers, for a brief period before further advancement, as vice-chamberlain. Edward Fiennes de Clinton continued as lord admiral. Henry Fitzalan, earl of Arundel, was transferred to the post of lord steward, and John Mason continued as treasurer of the household.

William Cordell was retained as master of the rolls. Gilbert Gerard was appointed attorney general, and William Rosewell solicitor general. Ambrose Cave was installed as chancellor of the duchy of Lancaster, and Thomas Cheyney and Thomas Parry became respectively treasurer and comptroller of the household.

Meanwhile, what Mason had described as the first and primary task of the new regime, the concluding of peace with France, was being carried forward by the commissioners Mary had appointed in September. They returned briefly to England after Mary's death, and then were sent back with their commission reconfirmed, with new instructions, and with lord William Howard sent along as an added skilled negotiator. Nicholas Wotton, one of the commissioners, was instructed to go first to Brussels to renew the treaty with Spain.

The exclusions from the council are almost as noteworthy as the inclusions. A major surprise was the omission of Robert Dudley, the chief surviving representative of the extensive family network fashioned by Edward VI's second "Protector." Equally surprising was the exclusion of William Paget. It did not occur to the Spanish ambassador that Paget would not remain as a key servant of the crown. Paget's professional career extended without a break back to the reign of Henry VIII when Stephen Gardiner brought him to court as his protégé. Paget was the most powerful and the ablest of the remaining Marian councilors. He was excused from the new council on the basis of his poor health, but he was not pleased by such consideration.[17] Several reasons can be adduced for his exclusion, any one of which may have been the true reason. Paget had written a harsh letter to Elizabeth informing her of the change in her household arrangements after the Thomas Seymour affair. Also Cecil may have acquired an acute personal distaste for Paget as a result of a strong suspicion of Paget's possible duplicity at Brussels in the arrest and subsequent humiliation of Cecil's beloved tutor, friend, and brother-in-law, John Cheke. A more important reason for his exclusion may have been a fear amongst Elizabeth's advisors that Paget was unduly ambitious in his grasp for place, power, and property. To anyone familiar with his career, he may have appeared to be a person who could not be fully trusted.[18] Beginning his career as

17. Haynes, *Collection of State Papers*, 207–10.
18. S. R. Gammon comments, with respect to the crisis of 1551, that

Gardiner's bright young aide, he had switched his loyalty to Cromwell, reverted to Gardiner in 1540, and then transferred allegiance successively to Somerset and Northumberland before enlisting as one of the chief officers of Mary's regime. Paget's shifts were in contrast to those of Petre and Mason in that Paget tended to anticipate changes, to precede them in switching his loyalty, and even to help precipitate them rather than adjusting to change after the event.

Paget, at the very least, would have presented a threat to Cecil's control and management of the council. He was too able, too experienced, too thrusting to be fully trusted. A similar problem, not in terms of administrative ability and experience but in terms of potential factionalism, was posed by Robert Dudley. He shortly was to become Cecil's first serious rival for Elizabeth's confidence, and with Dudley in the government as a member of the council the threat of polarization could have become an immediate danger.

Robert Dudley could be excluded from the council, but he could not be kept from the court. One of Elizabeth's first appointments was to make him master of the horse. Nor could his brother Ambrose, who became master of the ordnance, be excluded from the court. Still in other ways the Dudley influence was minimized. Some effort seems to have been made to keep such members of the Dudley clan as Thomas Radcliffe, earl of Sussex, and Henry Sidney at a distance—the first as lord deputy of Ireland; the second as lord president of the marches of Wales. Another Dudley connection, William Fitzwilliam, also was retained in Ireland, while Henry Hastings, soon to be earl of Huntingdon, appears to have been simply ignored.[19]

"Paget's own reputation for political trickery was such" that it is impossible to tell whether he had been plotting with Somerset or was betraying him. *Statesman and Schemer: William, First Lord Paget—Tudor Minister* (Hamden, Conn., 1973), p. 179. Gammon adds the further comment that "Paget was not at all averse to betraying an old associate," ibid., p. 234. Gammon, on the other hand, observes that had Somerset heeded Paget's advice he would have avoided the disaster which overtook him. Gammon also concludes that Mary would have escaped many of her problems had she placed her confidence in Paget, with his counsel of moderation, rather than in Gardiner.

19. Hastings, of course, was young, but his background might lead one to suppose that he would be the type of person to have been utilized in Elizabeth's government. He had shared Edward VI's studies, had spent a period at Cambridge, had country homes in the vicinity of those of Cecil, Parr, Russell, and others, and he was a Protestant. His two flaws were, first,

The exclusion of Nicholas Throckmorton from the council is more puzzling. He had been reared by the Parrs, and like William Parr had possibly been at Cambridge for a time. He established his country home at Paulerspury, five miles south of Parr's home at Greens Norton, which in turn was no more than a day's journey from Stamford. Moreover, both Throckmorton and Cecil were within an inner circle at the court of Edward VI.[20] It is not surprising, therefore, that the two men were intimately acquainted. Nor is it surprising that, in the burst of activity of the first days of Elizabeth's reign, the two men were working hand in glove, with Throckmorton handling many things at Cecil's behest.[21] Throckmorton's memoranda of advice to Queen Elizabeth give an impression to the careful reader that the two men had been consulting and perhaps collaborating prior to Mary's death.[22] Throckmorton's most urgent advice, as has been noted, was for Elizabeth to install Cecil immediately as principal secretary. Otherwise she should proceed with great caution. His watchwords were "defer" and "suspend"—i.e., to delay and avoid precipitate action. Matters should not be hurried but handled with care and in due order, step-by-step.

Indicative of consultation are the names Throckmorton put forward as persons suitable to be brought into Elizabeth's service. The names of all who were appointed to major office appear at one point or another among those whom Throckmorton lists as fit to be appointed. Of greater significance are names missing from Throckmorton's roster of suitable personnel. Paget, the two Dudleys, the earl of Sussex, Henry Sidney, Henry Hastings—all are missing. Most curious of all is the mention of Ambrose Cave among those proposed by Throckmorton, for Cave had no previous experience at court.

---

his marriage to Dudley's sister, and second, his intensely rigid Protestantism of a purportedly Genevan stamp.

20. Throckmorton had been a server-in-waiting to Queen Catherine Parr, and continued in her household after Henry VIII's death. His intimacy with young Edward began when he brought news of the English victory over the Scots at the battle of Pinkie. After this he was admitted to the young king's privy chamber and became a prime favorite. A. L. Rowse, *Ralegh and the Throckmortons* (London, 1962), pp. 10, 12–13.

21. See ibid., 25. Earlier in the year Cecil had been commissioned by Queen Mary to restore to Throckmorton his keepership of the parks at Brigstock. Ibid.

22. See the memoranda as edited by J. E. Neale, *English Historical Review* LXV (1950): 93–98.

Cave was from Stamford, Cecil's country seat. It is unlikely that Throckmorton would have to call Cave to Cecil's attention. More probably Cecil had already mentioned Cave to Throckmorton as a reliable person to have in the government.

If Throckmorton and Cecil were collaborating, it is clear that Cecil had not revealed his full hand to Throckmorton. Cecil had not disclosed to him, for example, the plan for a single secretaryship and a small council. Nor had he disclosed that he may already have gone beyond the submission of general lists of suitable persons and instead was ready to make specific recommendations for Elizabeth's consideration. Nor, apparently, had Cecil mentioned that he had no major post at court in mind for Throckmorton.[23]

Cecil had great respect for Throckmorton's ability—his quick grasp of issues, his efficiency, his judgment, his boldness, as well as his more subtle skills. Throckmorton's trial for high treason in 1554 had been a cause célèbre displaying the full range of his talents. By sheer effrontery, eloquence, and audacity in taking advantage of a legal loophole, he was able to win an acquittal from the jury—a feat seldom duplicated in the sixteenth century when a person of prominence formally charged with high treason had little hope of acquittal. Evidence of Cecil's estimate of Throckmorton was supplied in 1560 when Cecil, dismayed and discouraged by havoc being created by Elizabeth's infatuation with Dudley, was prepared to threaten to resign if only he could be certain that he could get Throckmorton, the only person he considered sufficiently competent for the job, into his place as principal secretary.[24]

There are two possible explanations for the exclusion of Throckmorton from the council. The first is that Cecil wanted no one on the council strong enough to be a potential rival, not even a person as congenial and as closely in tune (at the time) with his own ideas as Throckmorton. Cecil could scarcely have anticipated that by

23. Throckmorton was appointed chief butler and chamberlain of the exchequer before he was dispatched to Paris as ambassador.

24. Read, *Mr. Secretary Cecil*, p. 199. Further evidence of Cecil's confidence in Throckmorton is supplied by Cecil's placing his eldest son in Throckmorton's care at Paris. Recognizing that there was little likelihood that his son would become "scholarly learned," Cecil believed that under Throckmorton's moral and religious direction at the French court his son would acquire some knowledge of French and more knowledge of civil affairs than he would elsewhere. Ibid., p. 213.

1563, as the result of a series of misadventures, Throckmorton would desert him and become a close confidant and advisor to Robert Dudley.

A more plausible reason for Throckmorton's exclusion is that top priority was given to France. The first objective was to end the war with France, cutting England's losses, and achieving peace with a degree of dignity if not with honor. The second objective was to keep France off-balance and preoccupied until a firm and stable relationship with Scotland was established. "We only seek surety," Cecil was later to write Throckmorton, "which chiefly dependeth upon the liberty [from France] of Scotland."[25] To carry out the second demanding and delicate operation in France, it was urgent that someone of highest calibre be sent as ambassador to Paris. Cecil apparently thought Throckmorton was the only person capable of handling the job. Later, on October 1, 1559, when Throckmorton sought to be released from the assignment, Cecil wrote that there was only one reason Throckmorton needed to remain in France. This was "the necessity of his service," for, "all parts considered," Cecil knew not where "the like choice" may be found. The person Throckmorton had suggested as his replacement "cannot here be allowed."[26]

Embassies were never a prize to be sought. They drained one's financial resources, provided little by way of recompense, and cost one opportunities for advancement and financial profit at home. Throckmorton was no more happy with his assignment to Paris than anyone else would have been, and he constantly sought excuses for his recall. Unhappy as he purported to be with the assignment, he handled it with great finesse. Given what seemed an impossible task, his embassy to France turned out to be a brilliant episode in his career. His correspondence with Cecil at this time indicates that they were still working in fullest possible intimacy, confidence, and mutual understanding.[27]

25. Patrick Forbes, *A Full View of the Public Transactions in the Reign of Elizabeth* (London, 1740–41), I, 490.

26. *Calendar of State Papers, Foreign, Elizabeth, 1559–60,* II, 4–5.

27. See Forbes, *A Full View of Public Transactions,* I, 374–75, 379, 460; and also Philip Yorke Hardwicke, *Miscellaneous State Papers from 1501 to 1726* (London, 1778), I, 121–69. It was during his French tour of duty that Throckmorton gained the reputation of being the ablest intelligence man of his time.

III. THE ELIZABETHAN "ESTABLISH-MENT," 1558–1560

The new Elizabethan government, put together with such dispatch, had several striking features. The first was the absence of clerics as members of the council and its positions of administrative importance. There were no Wolseys, no Fishers, no Cranmers, no Gardiners, no Tunstalls, no Poles.[1] It was a government, for the first time, staffed wholly by laymen. Equally striking was the fact that the dominant figures were university-trained laymen, although this trend was well advanced under Edward. Also conspicuous was the religious complexion of the council which was positively Protestant. No fully committed Roman Catholics remained, and even "trimmers" in religion who had been too closely associated with Marian policies were eliminated.[2] The new appointees, to be sure, ranged from fervent to tepid in their religious convictions, but extremists of what was to be called the Genevan camp were not represented. The majority, men such as Cecil, Bacon, Mildmay, Knollys, Parr, Russell, Haddon, exhibited a firm attachment to the moderate Protestantism associated with Thomas Cranmer, Martin Bucer, and Peter Martyr. Moreover, despite a conscious break with the preceding regime, the new council represented a strong element of continuity, having a markedly Edwardian cast. Almost all members, including retainees from the Marian years, had had major responsibilities under Edward, and a significant number had served under Henry VIII as well.

1. Nicholas Wotton could be cited as an exception, but his role was peripheral, and, unlike Wolsey and other churchmen in government, he had not been a practicing cleric for years.
2. The new government was given an anti-Marian cast not only by those eliminated but also by those appointed. William Parr had lost his title on Lady Jane Grey's behalf. Edward Rogers had been in the Tower for his participation in Wyatt's rebellion. Nicholas Throckmorton, the new ambassador to Paris, had been tried for treason. Francis Knollys had gone into exile. William Cecil had virtually retired from public life as a gesture of disassociation from the Marian regime. At lower levels of responsibility, many who had actively opposed Mary were now brought back into the service of the crown.

Attention has been called by Wallace MacCaffrey to the several networks of family relationships—the Boleyns, the Parrs, the Dudleys, the Howards, the Cookes—represented at court: in the council, in the major administrative posts, in the household, even among the ladies-in-waiting.[3] Some families, to be sure, were less well represented than others; for example, the Dudleys and the Howards. The surviving Boleyns were not numerous or unduly influential, but with an intense family loyalty Elizabeth clung to what family ties there were. Other family relationships, including those between Anthony Cooke and his daughters' husbands, were important, and they take on added significance when analyzed in terms of a Cecil connection, an analysis which can most easily be made when limited at the outset to council members.

Thomas Cromwell's great mistake, two and a half decades earlier, had been to ignore the importance of developing personal support in the council, depending instead for support wholly upon his relationship to Henry VIII.[4] In 1540 when the crunch came Cromwell recognized that the council was his point of vulnerability, a vulnerability he sought partially to offset by surrendering the office of principal secretary and appointing his aides Ralph Sadler and Thomas Wriothesley to a dual secretaryship. This cost him some of the power he was able to exercise through day-by-day supervision of affairs as secretary. Nor did the two votes this move added to the council make much difference. Cromwell's error was compounded when Wriothesley quietly defected and turned informer, keeping Cromwell's enemies posted on the details of the inner workings of his administration.[5]

Cecil made no such mistake. He established for himself, in terms

3. Wallace MacCaffrey, *The Shaping of the Elizabethan Regime* (Princeton, 1968), pp. 35–37.

4. "Despite his pleasant conversation and capacity for friendship, it cannot be said that Cromwell succeeded at any time in attaching any member of the king's council firmly to himself." G. R. Elton, *Studies in Tudor and Stuart Politics and Government* (Cambridge, 1974), I, 190.

5. Ibid., p. 191. It is interesting to note that when Cecil eventually allowed his close friend Thomas Smith to assume in 1572 the title of principal secretary, he never permitted him to do much more than serve as his confidential clerk. Mary Dewar, *Sir Thomas Smith: A Tudor Intellectual in Office* (London, 1964), p. 3.

of personal relationships, a clear working majority of the council. Thomas Parry was a kinsman and friend with whom he had worked for a decade in looking after Elizabeth's properties.6 Ambrose Cave was a friend and neighbor at Stamford with no previous experience at court and only Cecil's favor to commend him.7 Nicholas Bacon was a friend as well as his brother-in-law. William Parr, marquis of Northampton, was another old friend from Northamptonshire whose views were congenial to his own. William Herbert, earl of Pembroke, was Parr's brother-in-law, able on the field of battle but with little taste for politics and clearly not a likely center of opposition.8 Francis Russell, earl of Bedford, was also an intimate friend whose country seat north of London, amid the interlaced county boundaries of the area, made him another not so distant neighbor. It was into Cecil's keeping at Stamford that Russell entrusted his wife and children while he was abroad helping fight Mary's war with France. His letters to Cecil at this time are ample testimony to the closeness of their relationship and of his affection for Cecil.9 Francis Knollys was a Boleyn cousin to Elizabeth by marriage but he was also tied to Cecil by several intertwining relationships.10 Edward Rogers, a brother-in-law of Thomas Cranmer, and Richard Sackville, a cousin by marriage to Elizabeth, were both reliable from Cecil's point of view. The holdovers from the Marian regime, including the earls of Derby, Shrewsbury, and Arundel,

6. As early as Elizabeth's affair with Thomas Seymour and again at the time of her infatuation with Robert Dudley in 1560, it was evident that Parry's personal emotional attachment to Elizabeth took precedence over a sense of obligation to Cecil and any caution Cecil may have advised.

7. Cecil's sister was to marry Cave's nephew in 1561.

8. In many of these relationships, the wives played an important role. Pembroke's wife was no exception.

9. On July 26, 1557, Russell wrote: "Be good to my wife and children under whose protection I do altogether commit them." A month later, on August 21, he wrote: "I must thank you evermore for your travail in my causes, which doth always continue as I perceive by my wife's letters." Haynes, *Collection of State Papers*, p. 204.

10. Knollys had been brought to court shortly before Cecil came back to London from Cambridge. He attached himself to what might be called for convenience the expanding Protestant coterie of Anthony Denny and Catherine Parr, a rather inexact designation for an informal grouping which included William Butts from the past and newer arrivals such as Richard Morison, Walter Mildmay, John Cheke, Thomas Chaloner, and William Cecil. During the Marian exile, Knollys was closely associated with Anthony Cooke, Cecil's father-in-law.

were to a large degree apolitical. This was also true of Thomas Cheyney, of Lord Admiral Clinton, and of William Howard of Effingham, a Protestant member of the Howard connection.

William Petre and John Mason were in a separate category from other Marian holdovers. They were trained civil servants whose careers extended without a break back to the time of Cromwell. Petre had been Cecil's mentor in the office of principal secretary and was a friend of long standing. He was a model bureaucrat who never betrayed a trust or sought to undermine those he served. Serving many masters, he served each in turn to the extent of his ability. It has been said of Petre that not a single harsh word has survived concerning him.[11] John Mason was not unlike Petre in temper and ability, although he was primarily engaged in ambassadorial rather than administrative work. He had been close to Cecil's most intimate friends, including Richard Morison and John Cheke, both of whom were exiles under Mary. Cheke, Cecil's cherished teacher and brother-in-law, had married Mason's step-daughter. Mason, moreover, had been associated with Cecil under Edward and held him in great respect.[12]

Cecil's potential support was not limited to members of the council. Other friends were in important administrative posts—such persons as Gilbert Gerard, Thomas Gresham, Walter Haddon, Walter Mildmay, Thomas Seckford, and subsequently Francis Walsingham.[13] On the fringe of the court were more friends: Roger As-

11. F. G. Emmison, *Tudor Secretary, Sir William Petre* (London, 1961), p. 296. A tutor to Anne Boleyn's brother, Petre was introduced to the court and into government service through her influence.

12. One possible source of dissaffection was William Paulet, marquis of Winchester, who was retained because of reforms he had initiated as treasurer. On March 15, 1559, the Spanish ambassador commented that Cecil governs in spite of the treasurer, saying, "they are not good friends." The ambassador added that he was doing everything he could to encourage Paulet's dissatisfaction. *C.S.P., Spanish, Elizabeth, 1558–1567*, I, 38. Paulet, of course, was in his eighties, and was flanked in his office by Sackville and Walter Mildmay. Mildmay was perhaps Cecil's closest friend, establishing his country home at Apethorpe in Northamptonshire to be close to Cecil at Stamford.

13. Some insight into Cecil's mode of operation may be gained from a letter to Cecil from William Paulet who wrote: "Now John Baker is departed this life (whom God pardon), I pray you to remember Sir Walter Mildmay for that office [chancellor of the exchequer], who is as [ably fitted] for it as any that I know." S. E. Lehmberg, *Sir Walter Mildmay and Tudor Government* (Austin, Texas, 1964), p. 48. Cecil did not need to be told to remember Mildmay, for Mildmay was his close friend and Paulet knew it. Cecil and

cham, Thomas Chaloner, Richard Goodrich, Thomas Hoby, William Pickering, Thomas Smith, and Thomas Wrothe. Apart from members of the government, Cecil had an equally intimate relationship with those who were to occupy the key positions in the church.

Writing of the Elizabethan regime as it took shape during the first months of her reign, Wallace McCaffrey commented:

> The new establishment was in an important sense a partisan one. Its members were, of course, partisans of the new queen; but, more than that, they formed a party because of a common outlook on the political world and common association for loosely defined but clearly understood ends. Ever so slightly, the crown had to yield its freedom of choice . . . and to accept a body of servants who were drawn together not solely by loyalty to the monarch but also by common political purposes that looked beyond the immediate interests of the sovereign.[14]

Unlike those who have sought to find the beginnings of "party" activity, even a conspiracy, in the Marian exile or in early Elizabethan parliamentary maneuvers, MacCaffrey does not use the term "party" in a technical sense appropriate only to a much later era. Nor does he place undue stress on the terminology he adopts. Still to use the words "party" and "partisan" to describe what occurred at the outset of Elizabeth's reign would seem to put the matter more strongly than MacCaffrey intended.

MacCaffrey speaks of the members of "the new establishment" forming a "party" because they had "a common outlook," were linked by "common association for loosely defined but clearly understood ends," and "were drawn together . . . by common political

---

Mildmay were contemporaries at Cambridge. They came to London within a year of each other. They both joined Gray's Inn. They were involved together in government service in the last years of Henry VIII and under Edward VI. Philip Hoby was certain that he could not count on the presence of the Mildmays at the Christmas festivities he was planning in 1557 unless Cecil attended. There were other connections between the two men with the Dennys and the Walsinghams and the Bacons. It is apparent that Cecil was compiling a dossier to justify the appointment of Mildmay, and that Paulet's letter was solicited for this purpose.

14. MacCaffrey, *Shaping of the Elizabethan Regime*, p. 42.

purposes." It is true that they had "a common outlook," but the common ends and purposes of their political activity were more "loosely defined" than "clearly understood." There was no carefully articulated party line, no real party discipline, and little semblance of an agreed upon overall strategy. MacCaffrey's "new establishment," it would seem, was at most no more than a loose grouping of persons ("our friends" was a typical expression), with Cecil providing whatever cohesion they had as an effective political force.

Everyone had ideas. What distinguished Cecil from others was his ability to coordinate ideas and purposes he shared with others into general plans, to establish rational priorities, and to devise means and proper timing for consolidating support. He seems to have been the chief political operative, the master tactician, the longrange strategist. He had friends and colleagues who shared his aims and who worked with him, but they did not constitute in any strict sense a party operating within a party system. Even enjoying as he did (most of the time) the trust and confidence of the queen, Cecil was never able to impose what properly could be regarded as party discipline. On occasion Cecil's powers of persuasion would fail. Conflict of opinion would turn into dissent, and there were a few within the circle of friends who became disaffected and defected to follow the lead of others.

The issue of Scottish policy, an issue over which opinion was divided and dissent quite marked, affords us considerable insight into the highly personalized rather than partisan way in which the government functioned.

In Scotland, as elsewhere, religious convictions and national sentiment were intermingled and had combined to precipitate civil strife. In the spring of 1559 "the Reforming Lords of the Congregation" in Scotland appealed to the English for help in expelling the French. Such an expulsion and the replacing of French influence with a stable Protestant regime was a keystone of Cecil's projected foreign policy, for it would eliminate a threat from the north and make the Channel and North Sea once again England's line of defense. Elizabeth, however, hesitated to respond to the appeal for reasons similar to the qualms she had had earlier when minor aid had been extended to the Scots. The Scots who were appealing for help were rebels, and Elizabeth was temperamentally opposed to abetting sedition. Not only were they rebels, they had associated themselves with John

Knox, for whom Elizabeth had an acute distaste because of his "blast of the trumpet" against the right of women to rule. Furthermore, Elizabeth believed that to aid the Scots openly could only increase difficulties with France. She also knew that nothing could be more calculated to aggravate papal enmity. Cecil was enough of a pragmatist not to be deterred by Elizabeth's ideological distaste for supporting rebels and for giving aid and comfort to John Knox. The two risks of the Scottish venture Cecil believed to be greatly outweighed by the advantage to be gained. England's security, he declared, "chiefly dependeth upon the liberty of Scotland." [15]

Cecil's problem in winning Elizabeth's assent for his Scottish policy was compounded by divided opinion within the council which served to reinforce Elizabeth's hesitation. There was much vacillation. William Paulet, marquis of Winchester, Henry Fitzalan, earl of Arundel, Wotton, and Mason were, to put it mildly, dubious. Bacon and Petre were sharply opposed and advised that only secret sympathy be extended. Finally, on Christmas Eve, 1559, Cecil was able to prevail in the council and secured a recommendation that a campaign be started in the north. Elizabeth still opposed any resort to war and yielded only when Cecil threatened to resign. In the meantime, Cecil's letters to Throckmorton in Paris contained a repetitive refrain. "The queen's majesty never liketh this matter of Scotland." "I have had such a torment herein with the queen's majesty." "The queen's majesty is so evil disposed to this matter which troubleth us all." [16]

Cecil used Throckmorton in many ways to speed the Scottish enterprise. The earl of Arran, next in line as heir to the Scottish throne and the only leader around whom the Scots could rally, was held hostage in France. Throckmorton arranged for him to escape and to be spirited back to Scotland. Throckmorton also made arrangements for James Melville to get across the Channel. In October 1559, Throckmorton returned briefly to England because of his wife's illness, but he allowed his departure to be interpreted as a possible "prognostic" of war to create uncertainty among the French of English intentions. The following year he repeated the ploy,

15. Patrick Forbes, *A Full View of the Public Transactions in the Reign of Elizabeth* (London, 1740–41), I, 460.
16. Ibid., I, 454, 455, 460–61.

utilizing a request that he be recalled in the same way. Meanwhile, in his dispatches, he had been pressing Elizabeth to intervene decisively in Scotland. He wrote that the French, having their hands full at home with domestic broils, were in no position to expand their Scottish garrison. "If now you lose your time and advantage," he wrote, "you lose your surety and reputation forever."[17] The troubles Throckmorton had in mind were those associated with the Tumult of Amboise which had immobilized the French government. Throckmorton himself had had a part in fomenting them, for he and the Huguenot leaders were constantly in touch.[18]

With Elizabeth's acquiescence, Ralph Sadler had been sent north to negotiate with the Scots, and in February 1560 the Treaty of Berwick was signed, which bound Elizabeth to provide an army capable of expelling the French. English intervention, however, was ill-managed, and in May the English were defeated by the French at Leith. Cecil immediately went north to take charge. By establishing a naval blockade, Cecil turned defeat into victory and forced the French to withdraw.

Cecil now discovered that a cardinal rule for a chief minister to a monarch is never to place oneself at too great a distance from the court nor to absent oneself for too long a period. On his return, July 28, 1560, he found that not even his Scottish triumph was sufficient fully to restore Elizabeth's confidence in him. While Cecil was away, Robert Dudley had been busy. He had capitalized on Elizabeth's mild disaffection prompted by the Scottish venture, and, at the same time, he had paid ardent court to the queen. Dudley had suddenly become a dominant figure in government. Even though his authority was not lodged in an official position, his power was apparent. Elizabeth seemed madly in love, and would give scant heed to public business. All Cecil's plans were jeopardized by Dudley's ascendancy and by the prospect that Elizabeth might marry him. Cecil thought once again of threatening to resign, but was deterred by the recognition that this time the resignation might be accepted.

To rescue the situation and to recoup his position as Elizabeth's first minister, Cecil may have resorted to some devious countermeasures. There are, to be sure, only a few traces of such maneuvers.

17. Ibid., I, 374–75.
18. Ibid., I, 379.

One is a report of the Spanish ambassador that Cecil had told him on September 11, 1560, under a pledge of strict secrecy, that the queen was conducting herself in such an indiscreet and intimate way with Dudley that he was thinking of resigning.[19] The report of the ambassador is but one instance of the tales that were being sent across the Channel and circulating throughout the capitals of Europe. Throckmorton, for his part, saw to it that Elizabeth got the stories that were being told about her.[20] Elizabeth may have believed that a divorce could be arranged to permit her to marry Dudley. Such hope, if indeed she thought in these terms, was dashed when Dudley's wife was found dead, having suffered a broken neck in a fall. It was apparently an accident, but how many would believe this if a wedding were to take place?

Although Elizabeth turned again to Cecil as her principal advisor and administrator, Cecil continued to have problems with Dudley who still aimed for the highest prize—marriage and crown—by seeking briefly Spanish support and then by gathering a Protestant faction about him. In 1561 Cecil wrote Throckmorton of the continuing problem posed by Dudley. With Parry now dead and Francis Russell, the earl of Bedford, in France, Cecil noted that he found William Parr, the marquis of Northampton, William Herbert, the earl of Pembroke, and Nicholas Bacon, his brother-in-law, "in this matter my best pillars." He further commented that, even so, he was "forced to seek by-ways, so much was the contrary labor, by prevention."[21]

19. Cecil begged the ambassador "to point out to the queen the effect of her misconduct and persuade her not to abandon business entirely but to look to her realm." Coupled with this request was further confidential information. Cecil said that, according to common report, Dudley "was thinking of killing his wife, who was publicly announced to be ill although she was quite well and would take good care that they would not poison her." The next day, the ambassador continued, the queen told him that Dudley's wife was dead or nearly so, and added that the queen asked him not to say anything about it. The whole affair, he concluded, is "shameful" and "scandalous." C.S.P., Spanish, Elizabeth, 1558–67, I, 175.

20. Conyers Read, Mr. Secretary Cecil and Queen Elizabeth (London, 1955), p. 202. For details, see Throckmorton correspondence in Philip Y. Hardwicke, Miscellaneous State Papers (London, 1778), I, 163–69. Note especially the revealing letter of R. J. Jones, Throckmorton's courier.

21. Read, Mr. Secretary Cecil, p. 210. For an account of Dudley's activities, see MacCaffrey, Shaping of the Elizabethan Regime, esp. pp. 93–141.

How may one describe these men of the council and the major administrative posts, as well as some who were employed in embassies abroad, a few who were related in other ways to the court, and still others who were to be key figures in Parliament and church? They did not constitute a "party." They were not political allies in any strictly partisan sense. They were not sufficiently linked by vested interest to be labeled a faction. Nor were they in any conventional sense a circle of courtiers attached to the monarch.

MacCaffrey spoke of the men who worked with Cecil during the formative period of Elizabeth's reign as "the new establishment." He obviously was not referring to a reconstituted church. When Mac-Caffrey used the term "establishment," he must have had in mind something approximating the meaning Henry Fairlie gave the word in 1955 when he redefined it to serve as a designation for a cluster of informal relationships of trust among persons at or near the centers of power.[22] Fairlie's use of the word "establishment" quickly caught the public fancy, but in the process was stripped of the precise meaning he had given it. In popular usage the term was commonly ap-

22. "By the 'Establishment' I do not mean only the centers of official power—though they are certainly part of it—but rather the whole matrix of unofficial and social relations within which power is exercised." The "Establishment" is a "pattern of social relationships." Power and influence which does "not depend on any formal relationships, but on subtle social relationships"—this is the "Establishment" at work. Henry Fairlie, "Political Commentary," *Spectator*, September 23, 1955, p. 380. This is quite different from Iain Macleod's hint of conspiracy in his petulant complaint of "the charmed circle" which, "although seldom mentioned in history books, runs like a thread through British political history, and anybody who does not take it into account has a serious deficiency in his political awareness." Auberon Waugh, "Waugh's World," *New York Times Magazine*, October 7, 1973, p. 101. Kingsley Martin also missed the point of Fairlie's analysis when he shifted emphasis from "informal relationships" to the absence of "democratic control." Martin wrote: "Probably the best definition of the Establishment is that it is that part of our government that has not been subjected to democratic control. It is the combined influence of persons who play a part in public life, though they have not been appointed on any public test of merit or election. More important still, they are not subject to dismissal by democratic process. They uphold a tradition and form a core of continuity in our institutions." *Britain in the Sixties: The Crown and the Establishment* (London: Hutchinson and Co., 1962), pp. 84–85. Martin may accurately decribe the situation in the mid-twentieth century, but his definition of "the Establishment" would make nonsense of McCaffrey's use of the terms.

propriated as a synonym for "power structure." This equation of establishment with power structure was unfortunate, for it shifted the emphasis from informal relationships to structures of power. In the popular mind the concept of an establishment also often became translated into a theory of conspiracy and underhand deals which was quite foreign to Fairlie's stress upon simple mutual trust as its distinguishing feature.[23] In spite of the way in which the term "establishment," as used by Fairlie, has become distorted, it still remains a useful concept for understanding the political situation at the onset of Elizabeth's reign if Fairlie's adoption of the word to denote informal relationships of trust is kept clearly in mind.

A cluster of informal relationships of trust among persons who had been or were to be near the centers of power, quite distinct from a circle of courtiers or a faction and not quite a party, had come into existence in the decade and a half preceding Elizabeth's accession to the throne in 1558. Involved in the interlocking relationships were kinship, marriage ties, congeniality, and friendship—especially friendships dating back to impressionable university days when ties that bind most strongly so often are formed. A common enthusiasm for classical studies, Protestant doctrine, and a reformed pronunciation of Greek had drawn them together. Piquancy and excitement were added to the enthusiasm when the "radicalism" of the most admired members of the circle of friends brought them into open conflict with Stephen Gardiner, chancellor of the university, who condemned their ideas as "subversive" of all good order.

It is clear that these university friendships, subsequently expanded during periods of government service, or before the courts, or within the ranks of the clergy, fall within the general conceptual meaning of the term "establishment" as used by MacCaffrey. For Mac-Caffrey mentioned that a conspicuous feature of the new breed of persons at or near the centers of power at the accession of Elizabeth was the possession of a "common outlook" which meant that they "were drawn together not solely by loyalty to the monarch" but by concerns which "looked beyond the immediate interests of the sovereign."

23. The word became so ambiguous and misused in political discussion that in the end Fairlie wished "the language could be rid of it." "Onward and Upward with the Arts: Evolution of a Term," *New Yorker*, October 19, 1968, pp. 173–207.

Whatever collaboration took place among members of this "establishment" was purely informal, being similar in character to the earlier collaboration of William Butts, Anthony Denny, and Thomas Cranmer under Henry VIII, although the latter were more on the periphery of power than at and near the center of power. In specific situations, probably no more than three or four of these "friends" were involved in the collaboration, but they were in a position to enlist the aid, if needed, of other "friends." The informal nature of the relationship meant that there was not always uniformity of opinion with regard to specific issues. There could be agreement on ends but not necessarily on means.

The men who worked with Cecil during the formative period of Elizabeth's reign were noted, first of all, for their unusual competence. Simply to review some of their names is sufficient to establish the point: Nicholas Bacon, Gilbert Gerard, Thomas Gresham, Walter Haddon, Francis Knollys, Walter Mildmay, Nicholas Throckmorton. Although Thomas Smith aspired to greater responsibilities than he was given, he was a brilliant scholar and a person of much more than ordinary stature. Few of the appointees could be called "clients," for most of them were too strong to be so classified. And even some of the weakest, existing on the fringe of influence, were treated more as equals than as clients. Roger Ascham is an example of the latter category. He never became anything more than Elizabeth's personal Latin secretary, reading Greek and Latin with her each day, yet he was an honored guest and the center of conversation at a dinner given by Cecil at Windsor. The conversation drifted into a discussion of teaching methods, especially those of John Cheke. The ultimate result of the conversation was Ascham's classic work, *The Schoolmaster*. Ascham later commented of the dinner that he was happy to be included "in the company of so many wise and good men . . . as hardly then could have been picked out . . . of all England." [24]

Instead of being "partisans" or "clients," a not inconsiderable

24. For an account of the dinner, see *The English Works of Roger Ascham* (London, [1761?]), pp. 191–95. Patronage, of course, was still a potent tool, and, apart from the "friends" who occupied a somewhat different status, there were many clients. Cecil, Bacon, and Mildmay, for example, were to be busy accumulating property to establish extensive landed bases for themselves, and each of them made widespread use of patronage to gain a regional status of major consequence.

number of those who worked with Cecil, both officially and unofficially, may best be described as "friends" bound together by common concerns and relationships of mutual trust and respect reaching back for a decade or more.[25] Most of them were linked by a common interest in humanistic learning, a common Protestant religious orientation, and a common geographical locus to the north of London. For some their relationship to one another was interlaced with family connections.[26] Moreover, most of them had spent a period

25. A glimpse of the intimacy of the relationships among these "friends" is provided by two letters of Philip Hoby to Cecil. "I pray you, take your nag and come to Bisham because I would fain talk to you. But above all other things, I pray you, fail not to be there this Christmas . . . to make merry with a company of our friends. . . . And I pray you exhort our friend Mr. Mildmay and his wife likewise to be there that the company may be complete." Cecil replied that he could not come for Christmas because his wife had to stay home with their 15-month-old daughter, for whom Mildmay had stood godfather, whereupon Hoby reiterated the invitation. "You know how long it is since I did enjoy you, and if you now deprive me . . . of your company at that time, I must think it is so great a sin as cannot be either forgotten now or forgiven hereafter; and in your so doing you shall be the occasion why I shall not have here him whom I so much desire and to whom I am so much bound—namely Mr. Mildmay and my lady, his wife. And yet, for no such strange thing or great cheer that here is to be had, but because Mr. Mason and my lady have promised to be with me, who will make us all merry. I pray ye, desire my lady to come and to bring Tannikin with her, and I hope so to provide for her and her nurse, so all the house shall be merry, and she notwithstanding at her own ease and quiet. I look for no *nay* hereunto, but remembering how long it is since we last met . . . to make amends for all that is past. And 'til then, I bid you both farewell." The letter is addressed to Cecil "at Wimbledon, or London, or elsewhere." In the end Cecil did spend Christmas with Hoby, although Lady Cecil stayed behind. It is not known whether the Mildmays joined the Masons and Cecil at Bisham. John W. Burgon, *The Life and Times of Sir Thomas Gresham* (London, 1839), I, 225–27; and Lehmberg, *Sir Walter Mildmay and Tudor Government*, p. 46.

26. The family connections represent an extensive network which can only be suggested. Cecil first married one of John Cheke's five sisters. Later Cecil's estate manager became Cecil's brother-in-law by becoming Magdalen Cheke's second husband. Cecil then married the eldest of Anthony Cooke's five daughters, with each of the others marrying friends of Cecil, including Nicholas Bacon, Thomas Hoby, and Henry Killigrew. When Hoby died, his widow married in succession two more friends of Cecil. Bacon's first wife was Thomas Gresham's sister-in-law, bringing Bacon into relationship with Gresham's not inconsiderable clan of wealthy merchants. Gresham's own sister married John Thynne, the builder of Longleat. When Walter Mildmay married Mary Walsingham, he gained Francis Walsingham as a brother-in-law. The mother of Mary and Francis Walsingham was Joyce Denny, sister of Anthony Denny, through whom was established a chain

37

of study at Cambridge, and almost all who were members of one of the Inns of Court were affiliated with Gray's Inn.

The affiliation of most of the conspicuous members of the government with Gray's Inn is an unusual circumstance, sufficiently unusual that one can only consider it to be striking evidence of an intimacy of relationship among them. Four members of the council belonged to Gray's Inn prior to their appointment (Cecil, Bacon, Paulet, and Russell), and four others became members after they were appointed (Parr, Stanley, Talbot, and Knollys). Four of seven major posts outside the council were filled with men who belonged to Gray's Inn (Haddon and Seckford, the two masters of request; Gerard, the attorney general; and Mildmay, the chancellor of the exchequer). Other important members of Gray's Inn prior to Elizabeth's accession included Francis Walsingham, Richard Goodrich, Thomas Wrothe, Alexander Nowell, and William May. In addition, six other influential figures joined Gray's Inn by 1561: Ralph Sadler, William St. Lo, Thomas Howard (duke of Norfolk), Thomas Radcliffe (earl of Sussex), Henry Neville (earl of Westmoreland), and Roger North (the future Lord North). John Fortescue and Anthony St. Leger also joined within two or three years. In contrast to Gray's lengthy list of twelve and more, the other Inns of Court collectively do not seem to have had more than five representatives in the government: William Corder, master of the rolls (Lincoln's Inn); Robert Catlyne, lord chief justice of the Court of Queen's Bench (Middle Temple); James Dyer, chief justice of the Court of Common Pleas (Middle Temple); William Rosewell, solicitor general (Middle Temple); and Richard Sackville, member of the council who had migrated from Gray's Inn to Inner Temple about 1534.

---

of family relationships at court. Catherine Ashley, for example, was another sister of Anthony Denny. Francis Russell, earl of Bedford, married Richard Morison's widow, and his son married Thomas Hoby's widow. To shift the focus, Edward Rogers was Thomas Cranmer's brother-in-law; Richard Goodrich was Thomas Goodrich's nephew; William Bill was Thomas Bill's brother; Matthew Parker's sons married the daughters of Richard Cox and William Barlow, the bishops of Ely and of Chichester. A conspicuous feature of many of these marriages is that a surprising number of the wives were as avid in their intellectual interests as their husbands, being well versed in classical learning and possessing considerable theological sophistication.

The major Inns of Court existed primarily to prepare and certify young men to serve as barristers, instructing them in the behavior and graces of gentlemen as well as in the common law and points of legal procedure. Such was the prestige of the inns, however, that persons of more mature years were admitted who never intended to pursue a course of study. The result was that an Inn of Court became a kind of club and common eating place, a center of conversation and fellowship as well as a place of learning, where mutual acquaintance and friendship were nurtured. After Cecil and his "friends" were recognized as having established themselves as the dominant persons in the government, it appears that Gray's Inn gained added popularity with admittance being coveted by many who sought to establish themselves in a place where influential connections could be cultivated.

A Cambridge connection was equally as striking as the Gray's Inn affiliation among those holding major posts in the government, and was even more pervasive as well as of greater consequence in the formation of early, intimate, and lasting friendships. Seven members of the Privy Council had been at Cambridge: Cecil, Bacon, Sackville, Parr, Russell, Cave, and William Howard of Effingham. This was in contrast to an Oxford tie in the distant past of Mason, Petre, and perhaps Knollys. At least six of those appointed to major posts outside the council had been at Cambridge: Walter Haddon, Thomas Seckford, Walter Mildmay, Thomas Gresham, Gilbert Gerard, and William Corder. Other Cambridge men of some political consequence included Thomas Smith, Francis Walsingham, Richard Goodrich, Henry Carey, Thomas Chaloner, Henry Hastings, Thomas Hoby, Henry Killigrew, William Pickering, and Thomas Wrothe.

It is true that the Cambridge connection of three or four of these men, in the absence of university and college matriculation records, is shadowy. The evidence for these few is mainly tradition as it is represented by a consensus among standard reference authorities: *Dictionary of National Biography*, *The Complete Peerage*, and the Venns' *Alumni Cantabrigienses*, checked against conclusions reached by researchers of the History of Parliament Trust. The problem is complicated by the fact that it was not unusual for sons of nobility and wealthy gentry, as Lawrence Stone reports, to take no degrees, to live "semi-autonomous lives" in private lodgings, and to study "often under their own private tutors."[27] Confirmation of their presence is often dependent upon a stray record of payment to a tutor. But even when the tie to Cambridge is based only on tradition, the tradition itself says something of the individual's group identification. A notable illustration of this is Anthony Denny, for whom there is an unbroken tradition associating him with St. John's College, Cambridge. Recent research has indicated that there is no time when he could have been at Cambridge, but he did have close ties of friendship and interest with St. John's men and he sent his son to St. John's.

The Cambridge connection becomes even more striking when it is recalled that Cambridge men, beginning with William Bill, who was summoned by Cecil to preach the initial sermon at Paul's Cross, were utilized almost exclusively in effecting the Elizabethan religious settlement, supplying almost completely the personnel of the episcopate, including Matthew Parker, archbishop of Canterbury; William May, archbishop of York; Edmund Grindal, successively bishop of London, archbishop of York, and then of Canterbury; Edwin Sandys, bishop of Worcester and then of London; and Richard Cox, bishop of Ely.

John Scory and William Barlow were initial episcopal appointees and were both of Cambridge, but as Edwardian bishops they may be disregarded for statistical purposes. They were a legacy indispensible to new episcopal consecrations and represented no free choice of the new regime. The policy of appointing Welshmen to posts in Wales also places them in a separate category. John Jewel was the most important early non-Cambridge appointee. But Jewel may almost be regarded as a Cambridge man by adoption. Parkhurst, Jewel's mentor and friend, had felt so ill at ease at Oxford that he had retreated to a parish, and Jewel himself was somewhat of an outcast at Oxford, which he found a lonely place until Peter Martyr arrived.[28] After the accession of Elizabeth when Jewel wrote, as he

27. *The Crisis of the Aristocracy, 1558–1641* (Oxford, 1965), p. 688. The problem, as it relates to Henry Killigrew, is discussed by A. C. Miller, *Sir Henry Killigrew* (Leicester, 1963), pp. 10–11.

28. For Jewel, see W. M. Southgate, *John Jewel and the Problem of Doctrinal Authority* (Cambridge, Mass., 1962), and J. E. Booty, *John Jewel as Apologist for the Church of England* (London, 1963). Peter Martyr, through his friend and colleague Martin Bucer, was a major link between

frequently did, of "our friends," he was referring to the predominantly Cambridge group. As additional vacancies in the episcopate were created and further appointments made, the new appointees continued to be primarily Cambridge men who had been within the circle of John Cheke's influence at the university.

It is important to remember when evaluating the significance of the Cambridge connection that the university community was not large and that the number of students was not sufficiently great to preclude general acquaintance and the development of friendship across college lines.[29] Most of the colleges were adjacent and even Jesus College, which was described as "remote," was no more than a five- or six-minute walk from either St. John's or Christ's. In addition to the relative intimacy of university life, one should also keep in mind when estimating the significance of a Cambridge connection that many of the students were barely into their teens. They were at the university during a period of their lives when the deepest and most enduring friendships are formed. One further consideration should not be forgotten. Cecil's own six-year period of residence at Cambridge from 1535 to 1541 meant that most of the Cambridge men who assumed positions of importance in government or church at the outset of Elizabeth's reign were his contemporaries at Cambridge either as students, fellows, or masters of the colleges.

The several characteristics of common interests, common background, common outlook, interlocking family relationships, associations developed during periods of apprenticeship, common institutional ties, and personal friendship would seem to be the most adequate description of "the new establishment" to which MacCaffrey referred when discussing "the shaping of the Elizabethan regime." Of the several characteristics, the pervasive Cambridge connection is the one requiring most detailed analysis if for no other

---

such men as Jewel, Parkhurst, Bentham, and Bullingham with the Cambridge Athenians.

29. It has been suggested that Cambridge did not have many more than 160 students prior to 1553, with St. John's being the largest college with about 30 students, followed by Christ's with about 20, Queen's with about 15, and the others with 10 or fewer students. H. F. Kearney, *Scholars and Gentlemen* (London, 1970), pp. 40, 56. These estimates seem unduly low, and perhaps do not take into account the presence of unmatriculated gentlemen commoners or pensioners nor those pursuing advanced degrees. Still, however one may qualify the estimates, the number of students was small.

reason than that it has received less attention than it deserves. Moreover, the Cambridge connection helps provide a greater degree of understanding why the Elizabethan settlement, both political and religious, took the shape it did.

It is important, therefore, to move back in time to trace first the beginnings and then the development of an intimately related group of friends at Cambridge whose presence in government and church was so prominent a feature of the formative months of Elizabeth's reign.

IV. THE ATHENIAN TRIBE AT CAMBRIDGE

"A tempest in a teapot," some would have called the controversy at Cambridge in 1542 when Stephen Gardiner intervened to insist that a stop be put to a new mode of pronouncing Greek. Gardiner was master of Trinity Hall in absentia, bishop of Winchester almost in absentia (he had a palace on the south bank of the Thames technically within the diocese), chancellor of Cambridge University in absentia (as was customary), and chief minister of the king. Since 1524 when Wolsey brought him to London from Cambridge, Gardiner had been engaged at court or serving abroad on missions of the king. By 1542 he had replaced Cromwell as the most powerful of the king's ministers. Why, one wonders, should a seemingly innocuous academic issue over the pronunciation of Greek have been deemed by Gardiner to be of such importance that it required intervention from London?

Discussion of the subject had begun quietly enough. The springboard was a dialogue, published by Erasmus in 1528, setting forth what he believed to be the pronunciation used by the Greeks of classical antiquity in contrast to the corrupted pronunciation of the sixteenth century. For Erasmus it was no more than an exercise in academic analysis, and he left the matter there. Two young fellows at Cambridge, however, concluded quite logically that the ancient pronunciation should be restored and put into practice. In 1535 John Cheke, fellow of St. John's and Thomas Smith, fellow of Queens', both 21 years of age, gradually began to introduce the Erasmian pronunciation in their instruction of younger scholars. Partly because of the prestige of Erasmus and partly because of their own youthful ardor, and in spite of the opposition of some of their elders who clung to traditional ways, they gained an eager following known as the Athenians because of their enthusiasm for classical studies. By 1540, when Cheke was appointed to the newly established regius professorship of Greek, acceptance of the reformed pronunciation throughout the university seemed assured.[1] Thus surprise, shock, and dismay greeted the 1542 decree of Stephen Gardiner, who had replaced Thomas Cromwell as university chancellor after the latter's "fall" in 1540, which reversed the Athenians' apparent triumph.

Gardiner's initial letter to Cheke requesting him to cease promoting his theories was followed by a remarkably harsh edict prohibiting any further use of the Erasmian pronunciation in the university. The penalties for disobeying were incredibly severe. The edict provided that any member of the university senate using the new pronunciation be excluded from that body, that any candidate for a degree persisting in a similar course be denied a degree, that all scholars failing to conform to the edict would forfeit their scholarships, and that students without scholarships who proved refractory were to be publicly birched before members of their college. In defending the severity of the edict, Gardiner asserted that it was sheer arrogance to presume to know the ancient manner of speaking, and contended that a departure from accepted usage fostered a spirit of restlessness and vanity and encouraged insubordination. Three years later, Gardiner was to note that "Oxford liveth quietly with fewer privileges than we have." He then added somewhat ominously that there be those who would that "we had as few as they."[2]

The edict was neither fully obeyed nor easily enforced.[3] Still Gardiner persisted in his effort to bring the dissidents to heel. On May 15, 1543, Gardiner reminded the vice-chancellor that he meant his order concerning pronunciation to be taken "seriously." There would be no wavering since he was determined to "withstand fancies even in pronunciation" in order to fight "the enemy of quiet at the first entry." Two years later, Gardiner again referred to his edict commenting that he had heard that it was not being obeyed and directing the vice-chancellor to enforce it. In his frustration, Gardiner was instrumental in placing on the university statute books in

1. Of equal symbolic importance was the adhesion of John Redman, Lady Margaret professor of divinity, to the Athenian cause and his adoption of the new mode of pronunciation in his lectures.

2. J. S. Muller, *Stephen Gardiner and the Tudor Reaction* (New York, 1926), p. 124.

3. Even as late as 1554 after the accession of Mary, Gardiner was still seeking to put a stop to the new pronunciation at Cambridge. Ibid., p. 260.

1544 a requirement that each student take an oath of full obedience to the chancellor and vice-chancellor.4

Taken by itself the issue of Greek pronunciation was inconsequential, a mere difference of opinion among academics. The immoderate response of Gardiner to the issue, however, is a clear indication that much more was at stake. Taken in context the issue of Greek pronunciation was evidence of a much deeper rift.

For the better part of a decade Gardiner had aligned himself at almost every point in opposition to policies and persons identified in any way with Thomas Cromwell and Thomas Cranmer. This opposition may have been in the beginning a consequence of Gardiner's wounded pride in having Cromwell gain ascendancy with the king rather than himself and more certainly of Gardiner's personal resentment that an obscure academic had been named archbishop of Canterbury, a post to which he had every right to expect to be appointed. While lines of policy were seldom rigidly defined, Gardiner became less flexible and more conservative at a time when Cromwell and Cranmer, although always cautiously, were identifying themselves with moderate tendencies of reform. Within this context, the issue of Greek pronunciation was of great symbolic importance as a tag by which one's loyalty and stance on other issues could, with some assurance be ascertained. It served as a useful tool, therefore, in a struggle for control of the university. Gardiner believed that Cambridge was worth a fight, and he believed that the issue of Greek pronunciation was a place to begin asserting his authority.

Gardiner was not alone in his view that Cambridge was important as a center of impulses affecting the whole realm and as a source of personnel to help establish and carry out policies in both government and church.5 Cromwell had sought to use the university to

4. J. B. Mullinger, *The University of Cambridge from the Royal Injunctions of 1535 to the Accession of Charles I* (Cambridge, 1884), p. 63.

5. Henry VIII's "divorce" provided an illustration of another way in which universities could be utilized for political ends. A somewhat similar resort to university judgment occurred in 1543. Convocation was engaged in revising the Great Bible. Gardiner was intent that certain translated words be replaced with mere transliterations from the Vulgate. The king was persuaded to take the project out of the hands of Convocation and refer the revision to the universities.

further his own ends and had believed that Cambridge was sufficiently important to become chancellor of the university himself, a practice that was to be followed by every chief minister from Cromwell to Cecil.[6] The controversy over Greek was no "tempest in a teapot." It was more than even a simple struggle for control of the university. It was part of a larger battle for control of England.

THE FERMENT AT CAMBRIDGE

Cambridge at the beginning of the sixteenth century was a small university town, known for its slow pace of life and the chill breezes blowing through its narrow streets from off the fens. By the 1520's and continuing through the 1530's and 1540's, however, Cambridge had become one of the most exciting and even fashionable places to be in all England. It was a place others besides Thomas Cranmer found difficult to leave. A decade after Cranmer's departure, it took a direct order from his father to get William Cecil to return to London. Still later nothing less than a stern command from the queen could prevail upon Matthew Parker to forsake his beloved Cambridge. Others, driven more by ambition, were not so loath to depart. But even those who looked for richer rewards elsewhere attempted, whenever possible, to retain their university connection. In this respect, Gardiner's long tenure as master of Trinity Hall was not an isolated phenomenon. There also were sons of the nobility and of wealthy merchants, with no intention of securing a degree, who nonetheless were eager to spend a year or more at Cambridge to share the stimulation of university life and to profit, according to their differing tastes, from the intellectual fare provided. The presence of gentleman scholars was especially noticeable after Cromwell took the university under his wing and a university connection began to be viewed as an asset at court and in government service for sons of an existing elite[7] as well as an alternative either to the

6. The line of succession—Cromwell, Gardiner, Somerset, Northumberland, Gardiner again, Pole, and then Cecil—accurately reflects the political shifts of the time.

7. Roger Ascham complained to Cranmer of the presence of rich men's sons who pursued their studies only to an extent necessary "to qualify themselves for some places in the state." J. B. Mullinger, *The University of Cambridge from the Earliest Beginnings to the Royal Injunctions of 1535* (Cambridge, 1873), p. 624.

46

church or to military prowess as a means of upward mobility for sons of the humble. While advancement in government service could also result from skill displayed as a lawyer in defense of the king's interest or from knowledge and financial acumen gained by success in foreign commercial enterprises, these paths of upward mobility lacked in varying degrees the social prestige conferred by a university connection.

The transformation of Cambridge from a sleepy and somewhat decayed university community to a lively center of intellectual excitement had been the product in part of the enthusiasm generated by the interest in classical studies which was first manifest in England at Oxford, then shifted to London with John Colet and Thomas More, flourished at court, and flowered at Cambridge at a time when it was withering at Oxford. Classical interests at Cambridge were fostered by John Fisher, who was appointed master of Michaelhouse in 1497 and subsequently became bishop of Rochester and chancellor of the University. It was also in 1497 that Fisher was appointed confessor to Lady Margaret, the king's mother. Through her patronage, in the years following, he was able to secure funds for the establishment of first a Lady Margaret readership and then a professorship in divinity, also for a Lady Margaret preachership, and finally to found and endow both Christ's and St. John's colleges. It was Fisher who induced Erasmus to take up residence in Cambridge, and it was Fisher, intent on encouraging the study of Scripture and popular preaching, who gave his influential support as university chancellor to the study of Greek and Hebrew. Fisher did not foresee the Cambridge that was to emerge in no small part as a result of his own activity, for the seed he sowed produced what to him was a strange harvest of alien corn. Even the two colleges he "founded, with the help of Lady Margaret, as homes of orthodox religion and true learning," became nurseries of Protestantism and, before the century was out, strongholds of a sturdy Puritanism.[8]

The new religious ferment associated with the Protestant Reformation was even more important in quickening the intellectual excitement at Cambridge in the 1520's than the innovations of the preceding decade. The university was an early center of Protestant influence in England. The developing Protestantism was partially

8. H. C. Porter, *Reformation and Reaction in Tudor Cambridge* (Cambridge, 1958), p. 3.

indigenous in origin but most of the excitement was derived from Continental sources. Animated debates at the White Horse Tavern ("little Germany," they called it) served as a symbol of the seepage of new Reformation beliefs and doctrines into the university community.9 The discussion of new religious ideas was a heady experience, a headiness heightened and compounded by the involvement of charismatic personalities. The names of Robert Barnes, John Frith, Hugh Latimer, and especially of "little Bilney," the most attractive of them all, were to become familiar to almost every English schoolchild. Dramatic preaching to which some felt called was followed by dramatic events. Charges of heresy, beginning to be leveled in 1526, were followed by formal examinations and formal recantations. Some were placed in custody for a time. Some fled to the Continent. Thomas Bilney, abject at having recanted four years earlier, in 1531 "set his face to go to Jerusalem" by embarking on a forbidden preaching tour which ended with his being condemned to be burned. Matthew Parker tells how he was drawn irresistibly to Norwich, like the apostle Peter following as a disciple afar off, to be present on the fringe of the crowd when Bilney was subjected to the horror of being put to death at the stake.

By 1531 an era was over. The White Horse group had lost whatever coherence it may have had. Bilney had become the victim of the fires of martyrdom. Thomas Foreman and George Stafford had died of natural causes. Others had fled abroad. William Butts,10 who later proved his friendship with the reformers, had left Cambridge some years before to become physician to the king. Thus, with the exception of Hugh Latimer who quietly acknowledged his errors in 1532, the principal leaders were gone.11 Other less colorful and

9. Participation in the discussions was informal. There was an ebb and flow of participants with only a few providing coherence and continuity through their leadership. But even this leadership was ill-defined. A significant percentage of participants were from Norfolk: Thomas Arthur, Robert Barnes, Thomas Becon, Thomas Bilney, William Butts, John Lambert, Matthew Parker, Nicholas Shaxton, John Skip, and John Thixtill.

10. Butts, from Norfolk and linked to Corpus Christi and St. Peter's Hostel with Skip and Parker, could scarcely have avoided the White Horse Tavern across Trumpington Street. Thomas Arthur was also linked to St. Peter's Hostel.

11. There is no evidence to link Thomas Cranmer with the White Horse discussions, and it has been observed that he was somewhat "remote" at Jesus College. Still, as a further indication of a break in continuity it should be

more cautious men were left, however, to maintain at Cambridge by the encouragement they gave to younger scholars a pervasive religious concern at the heart of their academic interests. Among the men who bridged the two decades in this fashion, in addition to Latimer, were Simon Heynes, William May, Nicholas Ridley, Richard Cox, who had returned from a tour of duty at Oxford and Eton, and Matthew Parker, who was in constant touch with his Cambridge friends from his new little "college" at Stoke-by-Clare. Still the initiative in the 1530's belonged to a new generation of scholars who were to blend an interest in religious reform with an intense enthusiasm for classical learning, especially the study of Greek.

TWO YOUNG SCHOLARS

The new era at Cambridge may be dated, in a formal sense, from the Royal Injunctions of 1535 and the supplementary injunctions issued by Thomas Cromwell as chancellor of the university. A major feature of the injunctions was a stress upon a return to the "sources." All divinity lectures were to be based directly "upon the Scriptures of the Old and New Testament, according to the true sense thereof, and not after the manner of Scotus, etc." Moreover, all students of whatever age and status were to be "permitted to read the Scriptures privately" and to "repair to public lectures on them." In the arts there was to be a similar return to readings from classical antiquity and to their "purest" interpreters. To facilitate the new educational thrust, each college was ordered to provide "two daily public lectures, one of Greek, the other of Latin."[12] Cromwell's supplementary directives further enjoined the university to maintain at its own expense, by donations from the colleges, a public lecture in either Greek or Hebrew. The importance of the injunctions was the encouragement and support they gave to a group of younger scholars who were eager to forward the shift in university studies represented by the new regulations and directives.

The two chief luminaries of the younger generation were Thomas Smith and John Cheke. Smith at the outset was the more conspicuous

---

noted that by 1531 Cranmer was engaged abroad in the "divorce" negotiations and was to become archbishop of Canterbury rather than to return to Cambridge.

12. The Royal Injunctions also abolished the study of canon law.

personality, Cheke in the end was the more influential. Smith is remembered by posterity as the author of the classic description of the English commonwealth, *De republica Anglorum*. Cheke left no major literary monument, but he did leave a deep imprint on many of the most important personages of mid-sixteenth-century England.

Both Smith and Cheke were 12 years old when they were admitted to the university in 1526.[13] Although Smith was at Queens' College and Cheke was at St. John's, they pursued their studies in close collaboration. Smith later described how closely linked were their careers at the university.

> We are of the same age and like condition of life; our studies have been the same and we are recipients of the same royal bounty; we have been engaged in continual emulation with each other in the arena of intellectual achievement but this rivalry which is wont to kindle envy and strife between others has hitherto only bound us more closely together in fraternal affection.[14]

The chief intellectual enterprise which bound them together was their enthusiasm for and encouragement of the study of Greek and Greek literature, an enterprise which included by 1535 a common interest in promoting the Erasmian pronunciation of Greek.

Smith was a "beggarly scholar," son of a herdsman from the vicinity of neighboring Saffron Walden, and he tells how in his extremity Dr. William Butts, who three or four years earlier had left the university to become physician to the king, came to his aid.

> I was still little more than a boy. I had no hope of friends. I was desperate from my poverty and helplessness and already meditated abandoning the university and letters when, on account of a report he had heard of a disputation of mine in the schools, he summoned me to him, quite untrained and unpolished as I was, entirely unknown to him, and ... bade me not to despair, and like a father rather than a patron and friend from that day gave me every help and encouragement.[15]

13. Smith was born December 23, 1513; Cheke six months later, June 16, 1514.

14. Mary Dewar, *Sir Thomas Smith: A Tudor Intellectual in Office* (London, 1964), p. 19.

15. J. H. Gray, *The Queen's College* (London, 1899), pp. 73–74. Two

The confidence of Butts in Smith was not misplaced, for he distinguished himself by his learning and eloquence as he moved up the academic ladder.[16] He was successful as a tutor and a lecturer in his college, and such was his prestige in the university as a whole that in 1538 he was elected to succeed John Redman as public orator, a post of distinction and honor.[17]

In contrast to Smith, Cheke was a child of the university. Cheke's father, Peter Cheke, was the second son of the lord of the 1100 acre manor of Mottiston, part of the honor of Carisbrooke, the chief fortification of the Isle of Wight.[18] Peter Cheke had become a university bedell in 1509 under highly unusual circumstances for he was not a university graduate. He had secured the post most likely through a family connection with Richard Empson, the university's high

---

other Cambridge men, Thomas Wendy and Thomas Bill, were to join Butts as royal physicians. All three were firm Protestants and used their influence on behalf of the university. Butts appears to have been the one upon whom Henry VIII chiefly relied both as a physician and a friend, and Butts developed an especially close relationship to Henry VIII's two most trusted friends—Thomas Cranmer and Anthony Denny.

16. Smith at Queens' College and Cheke at St. John's College both received their B.A. degrees and were elected fellows of their respective colleges in 1530, and their M.A. degrees in 1533.

17. The duties of the public orator were to write letters in the name of the university and to compose and deliver the formal welcome of the university to visitors of eminence. The office conferred precedence over other members of the university senate, the orator preceding them in academic processions and sitting apart from them at academic ceremonies. Smith was succeeded as public orator by Cheke in 1542 and, still keeping the post within their own circle, by Roger Ascham in 1546, and by Walter Haddon after 1550.

Smith was the tutor at Queens' of two notable students, John Ponet (B.A., 1533; M.A., 1535; B.D., 1547) and John Aylmer (B.A., 1541; M.A., 1545). Ponet was fellow, bursar, and dean of Queens', shared Smith's enthusiasm for Greek, was a skilled mathematician, and was deeply interested in the study of the church fathers. He became chaplain to Archbishop Cranmer, and then was successively bishop of Rochester and Winchester. He died in exile at Strassburg in 1556. In addition to his theological writings, he was the author of *A Shorte Treatis of Politike Power* (1556). Aylmer was tutor to Lady Jane Grey; an exile at Strassburg, Zurich, and Basel; and under Elizabeth archdeacon of Lincoln and then bishop of London. He was the author of *An Harborowe for Faithful and True Subjects against the Late Blown Blast concerning the Government of Women* (Strassburg, 1559).

18. For information concerning Cheke's family and early life, I am deeply indebted to Paul S. Needham's unpublished doctoral dissertation, "Sir John Cheke at Cambridge and Court" (Harvard University, 1971). Needham unravels many riddles concerning Cheke with deftness and skill.

steward. There were three bedells, one for each faculty. In addition to prominent ceremonial roles, the bedells had major administrative responsibilities to perform for which they received fees. From these fees they derived an income in excess of the stipends of the masters of all the colleges with the single exception of the provost of King's College. Cheke's mother, Agnes Duffield, was the widow of one of Peter Cheke's fellow bedells, William Pykerell, whose degree was in civil law and who presumably had been a fellow of Jesus College before he married. Their son, John Pykerell, Cheke's step-brother, also took a degree in civil law and became a university bedell. Agnes Duffield's own family had long Cambridge connections, including her father who graduated M.A. in 1472 and was given the unusual privilege of being exempted from giving lectures "for as long as he gives private instruction in grammar in Cambridge." Cheke's five sisters, daughters of Peter and Agnes, also illustrate the university ties of the family, for they all married men associated with the university.

An important connection for young John Cheke was his father's relationship to William Butts, the future royal physician. Both men were active within the inner-circle of the parish life of Great St. Mary's Church, sharing in rotation with a few others such offices as churchwarden, pre-elector, and auditor. After Peter Cheke's death in 1530, Strype reports that Butts played the part of a father to the young scholar, becoming Cheke's "great friend, counselor, and the encourager of his studies." Cheke spoke of Butts as "his patron," and referred to himself as "his son."[19]

A signal service of Butts to both Smith and Cheke occurred in 1538 when they were brought to the royal attention for the first time.[20] In October 1537 Jane Seymour died, and some months later in 1538 Smith and Cheke were brought to court to debate before the king whether or not he should now marry a native-born English-woman or wed a foreigner. The debate was not a serious one designed to aid the king to make a decision. It was rather an event ar-

19. John Strype, *The Life of the Learned Sir John Cheke* (Oxford, 1821), pp. 6, 26.
20. Needham informs us that Cheke had come to Cromwell's attention by late 1537, for several payments are recorded by Cromwell to Cheke for the exhibition of Cromwell's nephew. This suggests that Cheke was serving as the boy's tutor while he was enrolled as a gentleman commoner at St. John's College.

ranged to exhibit to the king the calibre of learning at the university. It is reasonable to surmise that Butts arranged the debate and sponsored the participants, since it was at his home that Smith and Cheke stayed while they were in London. It is also possible that Butts and some of his friends had the soon-to-be-established regius professorships in mind and were grooming Smith and Cheke for two of these positions. The debate certainly did them no harm, for when the regius professorships were founded in 1540 Cheke was named regius professor of Greek and the regius professorship of civil law was reserved for Smith who was sent abroad to prepare himself for the post.[21]

With Cheke's appointment to the regius professorship of Greek, it was clear to John Leland, Henry VIII's "antiquary," that Cheke had become "the chief glory of the Athenian tribe" at Cambridge.[22] The emergence of Cheke into preeminence does not seem to have impaired the cordial relationship between Smith and Cheke, nor did it diminish the prestige of Smith within the university. In 1538 Smith had succeeded John Redman as public orator, and in 1544, having been named vice-president of Queens' College, he was elected vice-chancellor of the university. Smith also continued to hold his regius professorship of civil law until 1552 when he was succeeded by Walter Haddon who had attended his early Greek lectures and who was one of Cheke's most intimate friends. Cheke's role as "the chief glory of the Athenian tribe" and the dominant figure at the university came, not at Smith's expense, but because of traits of character and personality which made him an unusually gifted teacher who was able to inspire students in their studies and at the same time win their affection and devotion. Smith was more the public figure. Cheke was more the beloved tutor, the model students wished to emulate.

THE DOMINANT ROLE OF JOHN CHEKE

Although almost forgotten by posterity, in his own time Cheke was a quietly charismatic figure who won the unstinted praise and

21. The regius professorship of physic was given to John Blythe of King's College, Cheke's brother-in-law. The professorships of Hebrew and of divinity were filled by Thomas Wakefield and Eudo Wigan.
22. Strype, *Life of Cheke*, p. 20.

acclaim of almost everyone. Students and friends attributed to him every virtue of mind and heart. To Walter Haddon, "he was not one among many but one who towers over all." To Nicholas Carr, who succeeded Cheke as regius professor of Greek, he was one who exceeded few in age but "all in learning." To Nicholas Ridley, he was "one of Christ's special advocates." To William Cecil, he was "one of the sweetest flowers that hath come in in my time." To Roger Ascham, he was "my dearest friend and master," the "teacher of all the little poor learning I have." To Thomas Lever, reporting to Ascham the recovery by Cheke from what was feared to be a fatal illness, Cheke was preeminent in every sphere. Lever rejoiced that the world had been spared the loss of "such a general and only man as he."[23]

Ascham pointed to tangible evidence of Cheke's inspiring genius when he reminded Cecil of Cheke's role as the begetter of the "goodly crop" of scholars at St. John's that had made the university famous. Ascham commented elsewhere that Cheke "did breed up so many learned men in that one college of St. John's at one time as, I believe, the whole university of Louvain in many years was never able to afford." On another occasion, Ascham observed that classical studies flourished "as notably in Cambridge as ever they did in Greece or Italy," and that Cambridge took second place to "no university, neither in France, Spain, Germany, nor Italy."[24]

Among Cheke's students at St. John's College, who were bound to him by deep bonds of affection, were Ascham, William Bill, William Cecil, Thomas Chaloner, William Grindal, Robert Horne, Roger Kelke, Thomas Lever, William Pickering, James Pilkington, Edwin Sandys, Thomas Wilson, and Thomas Wrothe.[25] But Cheke's

23. C. J. Lees, *The Poetry of Walter Haddon* (The Hague, 1967), p. 19. Strype, *Life of Cheke*, pp. 37, 88–89, 148–49. Edith Perry, *Under Four Tudors* (London, 1964), p. 98. *The English Works of Roger Ascham*, ed. James Bennett (London, [1761]), pp. 319, 339.

24. Strype, *Life of Cheke*, pp. 9–10. *English Works of Ascham*, ed. Bennett, pp. 241, 318.

25. Cheke was tutor to Bill, Cecil, Pilkington, and perhaps Horne, among others. Most remaining St. John's students attended his lectures, gathered in his rooms, and shared a developing intimacy of friendship within the small confines of the college. Ascham, the most effusive of Cheke's "disciples," is a conspicuous illustration of the fact that friendship, intimacy, and influence were not restricted to a formal tutorial relationship. Thomas Hoby has mistakenly been regarded as one of Cheke's pupils. This misinterpreta-

influence was not limited to St. John's. Students in other colleges profited by his instruction, example, and friendship, caught his enthusiasm for the Greek classics, and learned from him that one should not come to the study of religion with preconceived notions but "should fetch the whole doctrine of Christ" from "the fountains of Scripture" and next from "the primitive and apostolical writings which were the nearest to those foundations."[26] Among non–St. John's men influenced by Cheke, the most likely possibilities judged by their later connections would be Edmund Guest, Walter Haddon, and another Thomas Wilson at King's College; Walter Mildmay and Lawrence Nowell at Christ's College; Edmund Allen and William Latimer at Corpus Christi; John Pedder and Edmund Scambler at Peterhouse; and John Aylmer at Queens'.[27] Among students pursuing degrees at the same time as Cheke, with whom presumably he was acquainted, were Richard Alvey and Thomas Becon at St. John's, Nicholas Bacon at Corpus, Richard Cheyney at Christ's and Pembroke, and, need it be said, Thomas Smith and John Ponet at Queens'. Of his elders at Cambridge, Cheke developed a close relationship with George Day, John Redman, Richard Cox, William May, and especially Matthew Parker.

There are several indications of Cheke's ties to Parker. In 1535, when Parker was chaplain to Queen Anne Boleyn, Cheke solicited Parker's aid in securing financial help from the queen for William Bill. Bill, a brilliant student, could not be elected a fellow of St. John's until the debts he had accumulated as an undergraduate had been discharged and he had sufficient funds in hand to pay the

---

tion is derived from a comment that Hoby was reared in "Cheke's workshop," St. John's College. The reference is to the college, for Cheke was in London by the time of Hoby's matriculation.

26. Strype, *Life of Cheke*, p. 10.

27. Others who were at Cambridge during the period of Cheke's expanding influence included Richard Goodrich, who was admitted to Gray's Inn in 1532, Thomas Gresham, who returned to London about 1535, Gilbert Gerard, who was admitted to Gray's Inn in 1537, and Thomas Seckford, who entered Gray's Inn in 1540. (Two of Cheke's friends at St. John's—Thomas Wrothe and William Cecil—also entered Gray's Inn, the first in 1536 and the second in 1540.) Ambrose Cave, William Parr, and Francis Russell reputedly studied at Cambridge, but the dates are uncertain. Cave became a generous benefactor of St. John's, and St. John's claims him as one who formerly studied there. Francis Walsingham, like James Haddon, was of another student generation, but he was at King's when Cheke had become provost of that college.

"first fruits" of the fellowship. Parker was successful in his appeal to the queen and Bill's financial impediment was remedied. Shortly thereafter Parker became dean of what was called his "little college" at Stoke-by-Clare, and he enlisted Cheke to translate "into Latin with his elegant pen" the new statutes of the college. Cheke found Stoke-by-Clare a pleasant retreat and was a frequent visitor.[28] Still later when the college was in process of dissolution as a former monastic foundation, it was Cheke, now at court, who came to Parker's aid and helped secure a pension for Parker from the proceeds.[29] At a later date Cheke sought to secure Parker's advancement from master of Corpus to master of Trinity College, the new heavily endowed royal foundation.[30]

What is equally clear, as the network of acquaintance and friendship was developing at Cambridge, is that those most closely identified with Cheke were in process of becoming dominant in the university. The regius professorships and the tight succession in the office of public orator have been mentioned. There was a rotation of sorts in the office of vice-chancellor, but the pattern was broken somewhat in 1544 when Thomas Smith, although only vice-president of Queens', was elected vice-chancellor.[31] Smith was succeeded by Matthew Parker who had become master of Corpus Christi just in time to qualify for the position and was elected by an overwhelming majority of the regents, partially as a consequence of energetic campaigning by Smith and Ponet. A further break in the customary rotation occurred when Parker was continued as vice-chancellor for a second year. Thereafter the rotation resumed with the position being filled by men within the circle of Cheke's friends.

The near monopoly of the vice-chancellorship was the result of the important shift in the leadership of the colleges as vacancies occurred. William May had become president of Queens' in 1537; Ridley had become master of Pembroke in 1540; Parker had become master of Corpus and Ralph Ainsworth of Peterhouse in 1544; John Redman had become master of Trinity College in 1546, being succeeded by William Bill in 1551. At. St. John's Bill had succeeded

28. Perry, *Under Four Tudors*, pp. 58–60.
29. *Correspondence of Matthew Parker* (Cambridge, 1853), pp. 39–40. See also subsequent letters, ibid., pp. 43–45, 48–49.
30. V. J. K. Brook, *A Life of Archbishop Parker* (Oxford, 1962), p. 49.
31. The election, to be exact, took place just before the end of the preceding year.

Redman in 1547, and was succeeded by Thomas Lever in 1551. At King's Cheke became provost in 1548, and in the same year Richard Wilkes, a fellow of Queens', became master of Christ's. In 1549 two fellows of St. John's, Edwin Sandys and John Madew, became master respectively of St Catherine's and Clare. In 1552 Walter Haddon became master of Trinity Hall. Six of these new masters were products of St. John's, and all of them presumably, as was true of Parker at Corpus, were elected on nomination from the court.

IMPORTANCE OF MARTIN BUCER AND PETER MARTYR

The friends at Cambridge, who gradually came to dominate the university after 1535,[32] had been drawn together by a common enthusiasm for classical learning, an enthusiasm given added piquancy by the novelty of espousing the cause of reforming the pronunciation of Greek according to Erasmian principles. They shared the earlier interest in popular preaching and the availability of the Bible in the vernacular, an interest which had been whetted by the comment of Erasmus in the preface to his Greek New Testament completed at Cambridge.

The mysteries of kings it may be safer to conceal, but Christ wished his mysteries to be published as openly as possible. I wish that even the weakest [most humble] woman should read the gospel and the epistles of Paul. . . . I long that the husbandman should sing portions of them to himself as he follows the plough, that the weaver should hum them to the tune of his shuttle, that the traveler should beguile with their stories the tedium of his journey.

32. Gardiner's intervention in 1542 and 1545 to put a stop to the reformed pronunciation of Greek and thereby demonstrate his authority over the university did not succeed in arresting the influence of "the Athenian tribe." The election of Smith and then of Parker as vice-chancellor is one indication of his failure. Another indication was the frustration in 1543 of Gardiner's plans for the revision of the Great Bible when the king took the project out of the hands of Convocation and referred it to the universities. The royal initiative in securing the election of Parker as master of Corpus is further evidence that the influence of Gardiner even at court could be countered. The date of Henry VIII's marriage to Catherine Parr in July 1543 may be significant in marking the beginning of a sporadic ebbing of Gardiner's authority.

While those related to the Cambridge coterie were Erasmians in this respect, they had moved beyond Erasmian piety and were increasingly inclined to a sturdy Protestantism.33

Judged by subsequent behavior, Roger Ascham and Thomas Smith in their religious views were among the less sturdy of the Cambridge group. Although they were eloquent enough in voicing Protestant views under Edward, Ascham and Smith experienced no great difficulty in adopting the faith of the Marian regime. There were others who followed their example, but most of their Cambridge friends lived quietly, evading the issue, some in noncontroversial posts, some in retirement, and some in hiding, while a not inconsiderable number took refuge in exile. Cheke, to be sure, recanted, but his recantation may be cited as evidence of weakness, not lack of conviction. Others had recanted under threat of death, e.g., Bilney, Barnes, Latimer, and Cranmer, even though they later were executed as relapsed heretics. As a consequence of Mary's growing determination to search out and "punish learned heretics who led simpler people astray,"34 the "chief of the Athenian tribe" was especially vulnerable and was not permitted the option of quiet retirement or exile.35

It is true that these Cambridge friends articulated no clear common theological position, but it is evident by the esteem in which he was held that they identified themselves most strongly with Martin Bucer and Bucer's friend and colleague at Strassburg, Peter Martyr.

Martin Bucer at Strassburg was an apostle of unity and concord, seeking a middle way of reconciliation between Martin Luther and John Calvin, and succeeded in living at peace with both Anabaptists and the neighboring Roman Catholic bishop. To use later terminol-

33. Cheke, while appreciative of Erasmus, frowned upon the vogue for reading Erasmus. He felt that a person's time could be much better utilized in reading the classical authors themselves.

34. S. R. Gammon, *Statesman and Schemer: William, First Lord Paget— Tudor Minister* (Hamden, Conn., 1973), p. 216.

35. Cheke lured to Brussels, probably unwittingly, by his stepfather-in-law, John Mason. Then, having been betrayed according to common report by William Paget, Cheke was captured by agents of Philip of Spain as he made his way to Antwerp. Cheke was bound, gagged, lashed to a cart, and held briefly at Ghent before being shipped back to England to make a forced recantation. The following year he was dead.

ogy, Bucer was more Calvinist than Lutheran; or, to put it different-
ly, Calvin while at Strassburg had learned much from Bucer. As was
true of other Protestant evangelicals, Bucer stressed the supremacy
of Scripture while leaving room for the adiaphoristic doctrine commonly associated with Philip Melanchthon as well as with himself.
By 1548 he was a senior figure among the Continental reformers.
His theological leadership at Strassburg over a period of twenty
years incited respect throughout Europe, and his gentleness in personal relationships earned the affection of all who knew him. With
the presence of imperial forces threatening to inhibit his pastoral and
theological work at Strassburg, Bucer was pleased to accept Cranmer's invitation to come to England. Arriving in London in the
spring of 1549, Bucer spent some months with Cranmer before being
appointed regius professor of divinity at Cambridge, a position
which John Madew graciously relinquished.

No professor ever taught at Cambridge for so brief a period and
yet made so deep an impression. He gave his inaugural oration in
January, 1550, and he died in March, 1551. Although he was constantly ill and very weak, his lectures were widely attended and
eagerly received. His closest friends at Cambridge were Matthew
Parker, Walter Haddon, Edmund Grindal, and the duchess of Suffolk. The duchess had taken a house at Kingston, five or six miles
west of Cambridge, to be near her two sons.[36] Upon Bucer's arrival,
the duchess welcomed him to Cambridge at her home. She attended
many of his lectures. She helped nurse him in his illness, but nothing
served to arrest his failing strength. Bucer was honored in death as
in life. Both town and gown were represented in the funeral proces-
sion, reportedly numbering three thousand persons, which followed
his coffin to Great St. Mary's where Matthew Parker preached the
sermon. The memorial oration was delivered by Walter Haddon at
Trinity College. In London, John Cheke, notified of Bucer's death,

36. The two sons, Henry, who was fourteen, and Charles, who was twelve
were admitted as students in the autumn of 1549. Thomas Wilson had been
their tutor, and Henry had been sent to court to be a fellow student of young
Prince Edward under John Cheke. At Cambridge, Thomas Wilson continued as their tutor. They were remarkably precocious in their studies,
impressing everyone with their charming demeanor and scholarly ability.
Two years later they died of the same sweating sickness that had taken
Bucer. Evelyn Read, *My Lady Suffolk* (New York, 1963), pp. 85–86.

immediately dispatched a moving letter of consolation to Peter Martyr at Oxford.37 Peter Martyr was to return to Strassburg to establish a "petty college" for the English exiles, and for the next decade he helped fill the void among those who had found their theological identity in relationship to Martin Bucer.

37. For an assessment of Peter Martyr's influence under Edward and Elizabeth and of his role among the Marian exiles, see J. C. McLelland, "Calvinism Perfecting Thomism? Peter Martyr Vermigli's Question," *Scottish Journal of Theology*, XXXI (1978), 576–77. Cheke compiled and edited a volume of tributes to Bucer, *De obitu doctissimi et sanctissimi theologi doctoris Martini Buceri* (London, 1551).

V. THE CAMBRIDGE CONNECTION IN LONDON

The predominance of university-trained laymen and the exclusion of ecclesiastics from Elizabeth's government was the culmination of a long trend which had begun as early as the 1520's, suffering only a brief interruption under Mary when Gardiner, Heath, Pole, Thirlby, and Tunstal returned to positions in the government. Reformation principles which gave a greater role to laymen in the church helped transform the universities and facilitated reliance on lay officials,[1] but the movement of nonclerics from university to court antedated the Reformation in England and was encouraged by members of the government.

Thomas More is a conspicuous example of a university-trained nonecclesiastic in government. It was More in 1527 who recruited John Mason, son of a cowherd, who had just received his M.A. degree at Oxford, for government service, with the recommendation that he be sent to the University of Paris as a king's scholar to equip him for diplomatic tasks.[2] At about the same time, the Boleyns introduced William Petre, son of a tanner and another Oxford graduate, to the court. Petre may have served briefly as tutor to George Boleyn before being sent abroad to spend four years chiefly in France. In 1524 Thomas Wolsey enlisted the aid of Stephen Gardiner, son of a successful burgher of Bury St. Edmunds and fellow of Trinity Hall, Cambridge. Gardiner became both Wolsey's personal secretary and the following year master of Trinity Hall, a post he held, except for a brief period under Edward VI, until his death. Gardiner was a cleric and for many years bishop of Winchester, but he brought into his household two of his students who were not and did not intend to be ecclesiastics. One was William Paget, son of an obscure artisan, who also was to be abroad, chiefly in France, for an

1. See Hugh F. Kearney, *Scholars and Gentlemen* (London, 1970), p. 22.
2. J. K. McConica, *English Humanists and Reformation Politics under Henry VIII and Edward VI* (Oxford, 1965), p. 110.

extended period prior to 1528.3 The other was Thomas Wriothesley, son of a herald (presumably a maker of insignia) at York.4 All four men—Mason, Petre, Paget, and Wriothesley—were to rise from humble beginnings to high and profitable office in the developing bureaucracy, the latter two being elevated to the peerage. There were others, of course, who had less need of sponsors; men who were members of established families and came directly to court after spending a period of time at the university.

The listing of these five men—Gardiner, Mason, Petre, Paget, and Wriothesley—who moved from university to court in the 1520's is by no means comprehensive or exhaustive, but the listing does serve to illustrate a developing trend. Changes at court in the 1530's and especially in the 1540's sped the migration.

Viewed from the perspective of Elizabeth's accession, there are three important dates related to the movement of persons from Cambridge to London. In retrospect, 1541 was of great significance for this was the year William Cecil left Cambridge and returned to London. The marriage of Henry VIII to Catherine Parr which led to the reorganization of "the royal nursery" in 1544 was of equal future importance. The new arrangements for the education of Edward, Elizabeth, and a number of the children of the nobility brought John Cheke and others from Cambridge to court. The death of Henry and the assumption of power by Edward Seymour as Lord Protector in 1547 was a third significant date, for this shift in authority was the occasion for a new infusion of Cambridge men into the government at lower and middle levels of the bureaucracy.

CECIL'S FIRST YEARS IN LONDON

William Cecil was one of John Cheke's most devoted pupils.5 He was admitted to St. John's at the age of 15, and spent six years at

3. S. R. Gammon, *Statesman and Schemer* (Hamden, Conn., 1973), pp. 19–20.

4. Wriothesley may not have come directly into Gardiner's household. He and Paget were the same age, fellow students at Trinity Hall, great friends with Gardiner with whom they performed in a college play. According to the *Dictionary of National Biography*, however, Wriothesley refers to Cromwell as his master in 1524, and is described as a servant of Edmund Peckham in 1529. There may be a confusion of identity here. Wriothesley's uncle also was named Thomas.

5. All Cheke's students were devoted to him, and few could match the

Cambridge from May 1535 to May 1541, without taking a degree. He was a diligent student who enjoyed long hours of study. He mastered Greek sufficiently well to be appointed to give the Greek lectures in the college.[6] He must have taken time from his studies to visit the home of Cheke's mother at increasingly frequent intervals, for Cecil married Cheke's sister Mary three months after he left Cambridge. Nine months after the marriage, almost to the day, a son was born.

Cecil's departure from the university was at least partly at his father's insistence. His father was opposed to the marriage. Later biographers have speculated that the father was put off by the thought of his son marrying a "wine-seller's" daughter and sought to nip the budding romance by removing his son from the university. While Cheke's mother did continue her husband's practice of selling wine to some of the colleges, the Chekes could claim as good a lineage as the Cecils and a more ancient claim to a coat of arms.[7] It is much more likely that what upset Cecil's father was his dismay that the marriage offered no prospect of a substantial dowry. The father also, frustrated by his own lack of success at court, may have had something other in mind for his son than a promising academic career. Although a period of time spent at a university was a distinct asset for an ambitious gentleman, the father must have thought that Cecil had stayed much too long at Cambridge. But it is intriguing that the father had seized upon the Stamford grammar school and the uni-

---

extravagant adulation of Roger Ascham. But Cecil, if not effusive, had a deep-seated attachment to his tutor which survived the test of time.

6. Many years later when Matthew Parker, as archbishop of Canterbury, proposed the publication of a new version of the Bible, he sought to enlist Cecil as translator of one of the epistles. Conyers Read, *Mr. Secretary Cecil and Queen Elizabeth* (New York, 1961), p. 30. Cecil's second wife was herself an able Greek scholar and undoubtedly helped keep alive his interest in Greek.

7. Cecil's family were gentry but not distinguished. His grandfather was a younger son of a prosperous yeoman from the Welsh border who entered the service of Henry VII and established himself as a landed proprietor at Stamford on the Lincolnshire-Northamptonshire border, was elected alderman and a member of Parliament, became steward of neighboring royal estates, justice of the peace, and sheriff of Northamptonshire. At court he was sergeant-at-arms. Cecil's father, as a youth, had been at court as a page of the chamber, performing menial tasks. Later he became yeoman of the wardrobe but achieved little in the way of distinction beyond continuing to line his pockets.

versity as a path to advancement for his son rather than pursuing the course his own father had set for him in securing a place within the royal household.

The father failed to put an end to the romance and to prevent the marriage. One would suppose that Cecil would have offered resistance to leaving the university had he not himself been developing an interest in a public career. Furthermore he was faced with the necessity of supporting a wife. Without financial support from his father, this was something he could not do immediately. His wife, Mary Cheke, continued to live with her family in Cambridge, and their son was to be born in the Cheke family home.

Cecil was admitted to Gray's Inn in 1541, but little is known of him during the next few years. He recorded in a diary that he sat in Parliament in 1543, and in the same year his young wife died. Two years later, on December 21, 1545, he married nineteen-year-old Mildred, eldest of the learned daughters of Anthony Cooke.8 The next solid information is that, after the death of Henry VIII, Cecil enlisted in the service of the Protector Somerset in May 1547, participated in the Scottish expedition, and was present at the battle of Pinkie. By 1550 Cecil had leased the Old Rectory at Wimbledon, ten miles southwest of London, as his home. With his wife, his son, his sister, his wife's sister Elizabeth, his ward, another young man, and an unnamed gentlewoman, there were eight members of the family circle, plus twenty-five servants.9

One can only speculate what Cecil was doing during the first half-dozen years after his arrival in London. Knowing that he was of studious and serious bent, one must assume that he busied himself with his studies and his work. One may also conclude that he was busy making new friendships and solidifying old ones, and earning the trust of both new and old. One would also guess, on the basis of later relationships, that he was especially kind, solicitous, and helpful to women—a not unimportant trait at a time when there was a

8. Anthony Cooke was the great-grandson of a lord mayor of London, born in 1504 in the family's country home, Gidea Hall, Essex, and was privately educated. Cooke married Anne, daughter of William Fitzwilliam of Milton, near Cambridge, and directed his early energies to the education of his daughters. Anne married Nicholas Bacon, Elizabeth married Thomas Hoby, Catherine married Henry Killigrew. All were Cambridge men. All were friends of Cecil.

9. Read, *Mr. Secretary Cecil*, pp. 87, 471n.

galaxy of bright, educated, important, and influential women at hand. The relationship had to be brotherly rather than romantic; otherwise he would not so completely have had their trust. This role apparently came quite naturally to Cecil. With both his wives having numerous sisters and with some of them living in his household for varying periods of time, Cecil had ample opportunity to adjust to their moods and to practice the art of being an understanding brother. Cecil, in this respect, stood in marked contrast to Cheke who, with five younger sisters to do his bidding, could never really break from the expectation that the primary virtue of women was to be obedient.[10]

Conyers Read surmises that, beginning in 1541 when Cecil arrived in London, his father undertook "to introduce him by degrees into court life."[11] This does not take into account the strained relationship between father and son during the first two or three years of Cecil's residence in London. Moreover, in spite of his wealth, Cecil's father had few important connections. It is much more likely that Cecil was making his own way, moving within circles defined by his own interests and points of contact.

Cecil did not arrive in London friendless. His departure from Cambridge may have been at his father's insistence, but Cecil could have been encouraged to leave by the example of Walter Mildmay. Mildmay who was to be Cecil's life-long friend, had gone down from Cambridge the preceding year to join his brother as a clerk in the Court of Augmentations, a step which marked the beginning of a notable career in Tudor financial administration. A year after Cecil's marriage to Mildred Cooke, Mildmay married Mary Walsingham, sister of Francis Walsingham who went to King's College when Cheke was provost. William Walsingham, the father, was a wealthy landowner, a reader at Gray's Inn, and a successful barrister. The mother of Mary and Francis, as has been noted, was Joyce Denny, sister of Anthony Denny. Joyce and Anthony were children of a former chief baron of the Exchequer, and Anthony like his

10. This attitude seems to have created marital problems for Cheke. For all the loveable qualities reported of Cheke as a friend and tutor at Cambridge, one should not forget the streak of harshness exhibited in his tract, *The Hurt of Sedition*, written in response to the Norfolk agrarian revolt of 1549.
11. Ibid., p. 32.

father enjoyed the favor of the king, being one of the king's most trusted confidants. [12]

William Pickering, one of Cheke's pupils and a Cambridge friend of Cecil, was also in London, having come down from the university in 1538 to become a "daily waiter" on the king. Pickering's father was knight-marshal to Henry VIII. Another possible contact at this time was Thomas Gresham who had left Cambridge in 1535, just as Cecil was entering, to be apprenticed to his uncle John Gresham who, like Thomas' father, was a wealthy London mercer. Gresham, immortalized as the author of Gresham's law, married the daughter of another mercer whose sister was the first wife of Nicholas Bacon. [13] Bacon, who was to become Cecil's brother-in-law when he married Anne Cooke, had preceded Cecil at Cambridge. As a fellow student at Corpus Christi, Bacon established a very close and life-long friendship with Matthew Parker. When Cecil arrived in London, Bacon had again preceded him as a student at Gray's Inn. Bacon had been brought to Cromwell's attention in October 1538 when Thomas Cranmer recommended him for the town clerkship of Calais. Of more immediate significance as a point of contact between the two men was Bacon's appointment as solicitor of the Court of Augmentations in March 1540, the year in which Cecil's friend Walter Mildmay became a clerk in the same court. [14] Another Cambridge man and an early pupil of Cheke was Thomas Chaloner who became a "daily waiter" on Thomas Cromwell in 1538. In 1540 he went to the Imperial Diet at Ratisbon as secretary to the English ambassador, went on to Italy where he was shipwrecked off the coast of Sicily, and after many exciting adventures reached Spain at the end of 1541. In 1544 Chaloner and his father were granted the office of one of the tellers of receipt at the Exchequer, and the following year Chaloner was appointed one of the two clerks of the Privy Council. [15] Chaloner was to go north with Cecil for the

12. Denny was a chief gentleman of the Privy Chamber, a member of the Privy Council, and he was to be an executor of Henry VIII's will and a member of the council appointed for Edward.

13. Gresham's own sister married John Thynne, the builder of Longleat, who was an early associate of Cecil.

14. Rodney M. Fisher, "The Inns of Court and the Reformation, 1530–1580," a Cambridge University dissertation in history, submitted January 1974, p. 18.

15. The grant of office as clerk was signed with a stamp of Henry VIII's

battle of Pinkie, and at Chaloner's death in 1565 Cecil was to be his executor.

The real matrix of Cecil's initial two or three years in London, however, was Gray's Inn which existed not only as a school for the training of common lawyers (and gentlemen) but also functioned as something of a club after the fashion of Doctors' Commons for civil and canon lawyers as described by James McConica.

> Doctors' Commons was an informal association of civilians and canonists connected with the Court of Arches. It was located in Pater Noster Row . . . where the members owned a small house and shared a common table with other learned men outside the immediate profession of civil law. From its inception in 1509 it seems rapidly to have become a regular resort for men of influence . . . , and the membership record suggests truly remarkable possibilities for dining and conversation.[16]

This role of Gray's Inn is suggested by the fact that Thomas Goodrich became affiliated with the Inn in 1541 at the time of Cecil's matriculation. Goodrich, who for years had been the friend and defender of the reformers at Cambridge as bishop of Ely, certainly was not enrolling as a student.

Among the younger men at Gray's Inn, who had been at Cambridge during Cecil's years there, were Thomas Wrothe of St. John's, Gilbert Gerard, and Thomas Seckford. Older Cambridge men who were affiliated with Gray's Inn included Nicholas Bacon, Richard Goodrich, the bishop's nephew, Thomas Wriothesley, and William Paget. Thomas Cromwell had been a member of Gray's Inn, and Wriothesley and Paget, although having studied civil law under Gardiner, had joined Gray's Inn during the period of Cromwell's ascendancy.

The first years in London were quiet years for Cecil. If his diary is correct, he sat in Parliament, presumably for Stamford, a seat which his grandfather occupied three times. As has been suggested,

---

signature and witnessed by Denny. The preceding year Chaloner dedicated his English translation of Cheke's two homilies of Chrysostom to Denny. For Chaloner, see *The Praise of Folie, translated by Sir Thomas Chaloner*, edited for the Early English Text Society by Clarence H. Miller (New York, 1965).

16. *English Humanists and Reformation Politics*, p. 52.

it is safe to assume that he was an earnest student preoccupied with his studies.[17] After July 1544, when the "royal nursery" was reorganized and John Cheke was brought to London as tutor to young Prince Edward, it is equally safe to assume that Cecil was drawn increasingly into life at court. The new educational arrangements also provided the occasion for the migration of additional scholars from the university to the court.

CHEKE AS TUTOR TO YOUNG EDWARD

The marriage of Henry VIII to twice-widowed Catherine Parr on July 12, 1543, in a ceremony presided over by Stephen Gardiner, marked the beginning of a new wavering of royal religious policy. While the hard-line orthodoxy, symbolized by the Act of Six Articles, was not officially abandoned, signals began to be mixed. The removal of the project for the revision of the Great Bible from convocation to the universities may have been the initial indication of a shift. Perhaps no more was involved than the fact that Gardiner had irritated the king once again. Still Catherine was a positive influence at court, enjoying Henry's confidence sufficiently to be named regent while he was in France from July 7 to October 1, 1544. Gardiner at least regarded her as a real threat. An attempt to destroy Catherine in 1546 with incriminating evidence of heresy was brushed aside by the king after a brief consultation with the queen. A similar attempt to eliminate Cranmer a year earlier received equally short shrift from the king. Catherine's most important act, one of long-range significance, was to assemble Henry's children—Mary, Elizabeth, and Edward—for the first time in one household and to undertake responsibility for the education of the two younger children.

17. Late in life Cecil enjoyed telling of one prank in which he engaged while at Gray's Inn, the story no doubt being considerably embellished in the telling. Read, *Mr. Secretary Cecil*, pp. 30–31. One prank is scarcely enough to cancel out the picture of the serious student. It is of passing interest that Walter Mildmay in 1546, the year of his marriage to Mary Walsingham, became affiliated with Gray's Inn, perhaps at the suggestion of his father-in-law, who was a member. Previously in 1544 William May, president of Queens' College who was frequently involved in the service of the court, became a member. Among those subsequently affiliated were Alexander Nowell in 1549, Francis Walsingham in 1552, and John Cheke in 1552.

The young Edward had been established in his own household shortly after his first year, and the formal reorganization of the "royal nursery" did not take place until July 1544, a year after Catherine had become queen. The reorganization was precipitated by the need to make more adequate provision for the education of the young prince who was now six years old. The arrangements that were made seem straightforward enough to require no explanation. Richard Cox, who had been an unusually successful headmaster of Eton, was brought in to take general charge.[18] Cox was given the title of dean and made almoner to the young prince. It is not clear whether the title of "dean" was related to his position of general supervisor of the prince's studies, for shortly before Cox had been appointed dean of Henry VIII's College (formerly Cardinal Wolsey's foundation, subsequently known as Christ Church) at Oxford. This was a post not requiring residence and thus represented the pure bounty of an annuity.

When the school for Edward, which at any one time had no more than eight to twelve students, was fully organized in July 1544, John Cheke as a younger man than Cox and as the most renowned teacher in England had been recruited from Cambridge to assist Cox as Edward's primary tutor.[19] John Belmain, a Frenchman with strong Protestant convictions, was added to the staff to provide instruction in French. Others were brought in from time to time for special purposes or reasons, including the teaching of the manly or martial arts. There is a persistent tradition, dating back to contemporary sources, that the talents of Anthony Cooke were used on occasion.[20]

18. It is said that Cox was brought in "probably" and "almost certainly" at the recommendation of Thomas Cranmer. W. K. Jordan, ed., *The Chronicle and Political Papers of King Edward VI* (Ithaca, N.Y., 1966), p. xi; and W. K. Jordan, *Edward VI, The Young King: The Protectorate of the Duke of Somerset* (Cambridge, Mass., 1968), p. 40. A confirmed Protestant, Cox was an intimate friend of Cranmer and had been a chaplain both to the archbishop and the king.

19. The official designation of Cheke said that he was appointed "as a supplement to Mr. Cox both for the better instructing of the prince and the diligent teaching of such children as be appointed to attend upon him." *State Papers Published under the Authority of His Majesty's Commission, Henry VIII* (London, 1830-36), I, i, 764. Cheke was rewarded in a fashion similar to Cox, being appointed "the king's scholar" to the canonry and prebend of Henry VIII's College in Oxford with a stipend of £26 annually. Cheke also retained his regius professorship at Cambridge.

20. Paul S. Needham has called attention to such allusions. Four are noted

Cooke may have participated several times, but his aid was most likely enlisted in 1549 when Cheke was absent from court for five months as a result of his mother's illness and death, which was followed by his participation in the much-delayed and extended "visitation" of Cambridge. Cox at the same time was preoccupied with a similar "visitation" of Oxford. Additional instructional aid was provided by Roger Ascham who reported that he served intermittently as writing master to Edward even before he became tutor to Elizabeth in 1548.[21]

Soon after he came to court, Cheke secured the appointment of William Grindal of St. John's College as Elizabeth's tutor. Roger Ascham had been Grindal's tutor, and Grindal his favorite pupil. Ascham exploited his relationship to Grindal as an excuse to make frequent visits to court. Grindal, for his part, encouraged Ascham to initiate correspondence with persons he met on such occasions, most of whom were associated with Elizabeth. These correspondents included Elizabeth herself, Lady Jane Grey, Anne Parr, and Catherine Ashley, Elizabeth's governess and sister-in-law of Richard Ashley who was at Cambridge and, like Ascham, was a fellow of St. John's.[22] When Grindal died of the plague in January 1548, it was Ascham who replaced him as tutor to Elizabeth. This was accomplished at Elizabeth's insistence and with the support of Cheke.[23]

In addition to those who were at court instructing the royal children and the children of nobility who joined Edward and Elizabeth as fellow pupils, other members of the Athenian tribe at Cambridge were engaged as tutors elsewhere. John Aylmer of Norfolk, who had been sent to Cambridge at the expense of Henry Grey, marquis of Dorset, was installed by the marquis as his private chaplain and

---

in *Literary Remains of Edward VI*, ed. J. G. Nichols (London, 1857), pp. l–li. For additional allusions, see Thomas Wilson, *The Rule of Reason* (1551); John Cheke, *De pronuntiatione Græcæ potissimum linguæ cum Stephano Wintoniensi episcopo* (Basle, 1555); and John Parkhurst, *J. Parkhursti ludicra siue epigrammata iuvenilia* (1573), written years before its publication.

21. Lawrence V. Ryan, *Roger Ascham* (Stanford, 1963), p. 107.

22. Ibid., pp. 103–4. Catherine Ashley was a sister of Anthony Denny's wife.

23. Princess Mary, of course, was a young woman who no longer needed a tutor, but Catherine Parr encouraged her to continue her scholarly interests, setting for her specifically the task of translating a portion of Erasmus' *Paraphrases of the New Testament*.

tutor to his children, including Lady Jane Grey, one of the most brilliant of the whole coterie of feminine scholars that was so conspicuous a feature of the time. Aylmer was succeeded in this post by James Haddon, younger brother of Walter Haddon, who previously had been in the Suffolk household. Thomas Wilson of King's College, on Cheke's recommendation, became tutor to the two Brandon boys, the precocious sons of Catherine Willoughby, the duchess of Suffolk.

In retrospect the arrangements for the education of Edward and Elizabeth may seem to have been a perfectly natural consequence of the introduction of Catherine Parr as queen into the life of the court. She had taken an immediate interest in the children and their education, and both the personnel and the shape of the new educational program ran along lines the new queen would have favored.

Catherine Parr's mother had been left a widow at the age of 22, and instead of remarrying she had devoted her income and considerable energies to an ambitious program of education for her three children—William, Catherine, and Anne. All were apt pupils. William Parr, the future marquis of Northampton, went to Cambridge for a period of study, and both Catherine and Anne developed a love of learning and became good scholars. Catherine had a good command of Latin, was fluent in French, and was familiar with Greek. Catherine might be called a child bride. Although the date of her marriage is not known, she was widowed at seventeen, having married an "ancient" man with "a distracted memory." Another arranged marriage made Catherine the third wife of Lord Latimer. She was about to marry for the first time a man of her own choice, Thomas Seymour, when Henry VIII selected her as his sixth and final bride. Catherine Parr's sister Anne meanwhile had entered Queen Jane Seymour's household, had assisted at Edward's christening, and had married William Herbert who was to become the earl of Pembroke.

One of Catherine Parr's close friends (one of only seventeen present at her wedding to the king) was another child bride, the duchess of Suffolk, a young woman of beauty, charm, intelligence, doughty integrity, and ready wit. At the age of eight or nine, the future duchess of Suffolk, Catherine, baroness Willoughby, had been left as ward of Charles Brandon, duke of Suffolk. As the duke's ward, she was reared and educated with his two daughters, one of whom was about the same age, the other about three years older. In the spring of 1533 the duke's older daughter married the earl of Dorset and shortly thereafter her mother, sister of Henry VIII, died. In September 1533 the 48-year-old duke married his 14- or 15-year-old ward, Catherine Willoughby.[24] The duke and his new wife by the late 1530's had become Protestants. The young duchess had been greatly impressed by Hugh Latimer who began preaching at court in 1530. For four or five years, until his death in 1542, the Scottish Protestant, Alexander Seton, had been the Suffolk household chaplain. He was replaced by John Parkhurst, a Protestant refugee from Oxford who identified himself with the Athenians at Cambridge. Catherine Parr was reported to have become infected with Protestant heresies by Catherine Willoughby, the duchess of Suffolk,[25] a rumor given credence by the fact that John Parkhurst became Catherine Parr's domestic chaplain when she married Henry VIII. It is not unlikely, however, that Catherine Parr was a Protestant by inclination prior to her marriage.[26]

Despite the new queen's influence, decisions were not made without the king's consent. The reorganization of the "royal nursery" and arrangements for Edward's future education were matters of major concern to Henry. The reorganization was not put into effect until the royal approval had been received prior to the king's departure for France. The education of the prince was of equal concern to others who recognized how decisive it could be for the future. The formative process of education, by shaping the character and views of young Edward, would do much to determine what was in store for England. The stakes were high. The selection of the pri-

24. Four years later, having become the father of two sons by Catherine Willoughby, the duke stood as godfather to Henry VIII's long-desired son, Edward.

25. Evelyn Read, *My Lady Suffolk* (New York, 1963), p. 61. The intimacy of the relationship between the two women is indicated by Catherine Parr's dying request that the duchess of Suffolk undertake the care of her only child.

26. It has been suggested that Catherine Parr's *The Lamentation of a Sinner*, printed in 1547 at the request of the duchess of Suffolk and Catherine's brother William Parr and with a commendatory preface by William Cecil, exhibits little that can be described as specifically Protestant. See Mc-Conica, *English Humanists and Reformation Politics*, pp. 228–32. It should be remembered, however, that one could scarcely expect Henry VIII's wife to write anything that could be identified as specifically Protestant while Henry was still living.

mary tutor for the prince was much too important to be left to chance.

According to Strype, it was Dr. William Butts, the king's physician, who recommended Cheke's appointment, but Cheke's name would have occurred to many. As the most famous and admired teacher in England he would seem to have needed no recommendation. Given Cheke's reputation, plus the fact that Cheke was known to the king and that Butts, who had daily access to the king, was urging Cheke's appointment, there would seem to be little need to explore any further the background of his appointment. Paul Needham, however, has pointed out how nothing was taken for granted by Butts. Much careful planning preceded and prepared the way for Cheke's move from Cambridge to London.

A key figure who may have been involved in devising the strategy was Anthony Denny, chief gentleman of the Privy Chamber and Henry's most trusted confidant during the king's last years. Denny had attended St. Paul's School in London, and was deeply interested in classical learning. Both he and his wife were convinced Protestants, and his affinity with the Athenians is suggested by the fact that he sent his son to St. John's. Indeed, so closely was he identified with the Cambridge group that it has been generally but mistakenly assumed that he himself spent some time at St. John's. Needham suggests that with so much at stake Butts had enlisted Denny's support in securing Cheke's appointment as tutor to Edward. Needham finds credence for this supposition by noting how closely and how often Butts and Denny worked together. He cites their joint effort to thwart the plot hatched against Cranmer in 1543, their close collaboration on behalf of Richard Turner when he was placed in danger by a false accusation of sedition, and their success in obtaining the king's pardon of Ralph Morice's chaplain.[27]

Cheke knew he was to be appointed Edward's tutor by June 10, 1544, a month before the official announcement in July. Almost a year earlier, Cheke had been engaged in a project designed to please the king and gain his favor by a display of scholarship. The project

27. *The Acts and Monuments of John Foxe*, ed. S. R. Catley (London, 1837–41), VIII, 31–34; *Letters and Papers . . . of Henry VIII* (London, 1862–1932), XXI, ii, 288–89; *Narratives of the Days of the Reformation*, ed. J. G. Nichols (Westminster, 1859), pp. 253, 254–58; Jasper Ridley, *Thomas Cranmer* (Oxford, 1962), p. 244.

took the form of a Latin translation of two previously unprinted homilies of St. John Chrysostom to be presented as a 1543 Christmas gift to the king.[28] Cheke included in the volume the original Greek text and a fulsome dedication to Henry. It was beautifully printed by Reyner Wolfe, a Strassburg native active as an emissary of Cranmer and Cromwell, who came to England in 1537 and set himself up as a bookseller. Wolfe did not begin printing until 1542, and he had printed only two items prior to the printing of Cheke's Christmas gift to the king which was completed in August 1543. For an extended period prior to August, Cheke was with Butts in London, presumably putting the final touches on the manuscript and seeing it through the press.[29]

Cheke continued his quest for Henry's favor by presenting him with a Latin translation of an unpublished military treatise attributed to Leo VI, the Byzantine emperor. The treatise was not printed, perhaps because of the pressure of time, since the outbreak of war with Scotland gave the treatise a certain timeliness. Or the urgency in making the presentation to the king may have been related to the uncertain timing of the impending decision with regard to Edward's education. The presentation copy was in Cheke's elegant italic hand. The dedication was dated April 5, 1544. Cheke mentioned in the dedication that the treatise might be especially useful to Henry at this time. A month later Cheke was named as "the king's scholar" to the canonry and prebend of Henry VIII's College in Oxford, apparently to provide Cheke with a stipend for his subsequent service as tutor to the prince, the post to which he was appointed shortly thereafter.

Whatever the circumstances which brought him there—the simple recommendation of Butts, a quiet campaign engineered by Butts

28. Information concerning this project and Cheke's subsequent translation of a Byzantine military treatise is drawn from Needham's unpublished 1971 Harvard dissertation.

29. The question of how and by whom the printing of the homilies was financed, Needham suggests, is an interesting one. This was the first piece of sustained Greek printing in England. Wolfe, although a beginner in the printing trade, was the first printer in England to possess a full complement of Greek type. Importing the type from abroad involved a major investment. Nor was any expense spared in the elaborate printing and binding. Even under ordinary circumstances, a Latin and Greek edition of two of Chrysostom's homilies could scarcely be expected to turn a profit.

with the possible collaboration of Denny, Cranmer, and Cox, the influence of Catherine Parr, or Cheke's own wooing of the king—by July 1544 Cheke had made the transition from Cambridge to London.

CAMBRIDGE RECRUITS UNDER EDWARD VI

When Henry VIII died in the early morning of January 28, 1547, with Anthony Denny in attendance and Thomas Cranmer summoned to give words of comfort and assurance, the throne passed to Edward VI, a child nine years of age. The care of the young king and of the kingdom was placed by Henry's recently drafted will in the hands of a council of regency dominated by Protestant sympathizers.[30] Edward Seymour, earl of Hertford, acted with dispatch to secure the person of his nephew, and one of the first acts of the council was to place Edward in the custody of his uncle and two chief gentlemen of Henry VIII's Privy Chamber—Anthony Denny and William Herbert. Seymour, a rallying figure for Protestants, was the only likely possibility to take charge of the government. After having been created duke of Somerset, he was eased with speed and audacity into the position of Lord Protector. The maneuvers which effected this transference of power were carried out with the smoothness and efficiency of an experienced bureaucrat by William Paget, the ablest and politically most sophisticated member of the council. Paget had the additional advantage of being with and acting for Henry VIII during the last weeks of his life, a fact which gave him credibility when he assumed the role of interpreter of the dying king's intentions, wishes, and desires. Paget also, now that it was safe to do so, was able to recall that "he had been a keen Protestant in the early days at Cambridge."[31]

30. By a quirk of fate the conservative influence of the Howards was dealt a lethal blow by the folly of the earl of Surrey who had been arrested for high treason on December 2, 1546, and executed on January 17. His father, the elderly duke of Norfolk, was in the Tower awaiting execution when the king died. Stephen Gardiner's ill-timed quarrel with the king was at least partially responsible for eliminating him as a prospective member of the council with the result that religious conservatism had no effective leadership in the government.

31. A. G. Dickens, *The English Reformation* (New York, 1964), p. 201.

A conspicuous feature of the new council (the 16 "executors" of Henry VIII's will plus the 12 designated as their "assistants") was the number of members who had been formally educated.

It is wholly safe to say that never before had the principal officers of state as a body enjoyed as high a degree of literacy and of intellectual competence. . . . It is certain that just over half (fifteen) of the councillors had matriculated in one of the universities or Inns of Court, and it is possible that four more, including Somerset, regarding whom the evidence is very unreliable, should be added to this number. . . .

Evidence, rather casually collected, from the diplomatic sources suggests that at least eight of the original council, Somerset being one, spoke French with an ease which satisfied even the French ambassador, and at least nine more certainly read and understood the language. And a considerable number of officers of state were cultivated and bookish men. . . .

This literate and cultivated taste . . . was even more marked amongst junior officers of state and public servants of the second rank.[32]

Given the interest in learning and the Protestant inclination of most members of the new government, the transfer of power from Henry VIII to the Protector Somerset enhanced and consolidated the position of the youthful coterie from Cambridge at court.

Somerset was the chief patron of the Cambridge men, but there were others, including John Dudley, viscount Lisle and shortly to be made earl of Warwick, who were ready to forward their interests. Thomas Cranmer headed the list of Henry's executors, and the list included both Anthony Denny, Walter Mildmay's father-in-law, and William Herbert, Catherine Parr's brother-in-law. William Parr had his own personal contact with the Athenian tribe at Cambridge and, as the queen's brother, had been made earl of Essex, sworn to the Privy Council, and named one of the assistants to the council of regency, all of whom were incorporated within an en-

32. Jordan, *Edward VI, the Young King: The Protectorate of the Duke of Somerset*, pp. 83–85. For further discussion of the character of the Edwardian council, see D. E. Hoak, *The King's Council in the Reign of Edward VI* (New York: Cambridge University Press, 1976), pp. 80–90, 263–64.

larged council. William Butts, who had played such an influential role as the king's physician, was dead. But two other Cambridge men, Thomas Wendy and Thomas Bill (William Bill's brother), were royal physicians in close touch with the younger Cambridge group and were in a position to be helpful. In addition John Cheke was now in a post of strategic importance. As the royal tutor he was always at young Edward's side, and the tie between teacher and pupil steadily grew stronger. Cheke was a person to be taken into account and cultivated by those who aspired to royal favor.[33]

Although Cecil did become "the wheel-horse of the administration" during the last year and a half of Edward VI's life,[34] he must be regarded as something of a late-bloomer. It was not until the accession of Elizabeth that he emerged as the central figure of the circle of friends brought together initially at Cambridge. He was overshadowed at the outset of Edward's reign by Cheke and Smith, and two or three other members of what Leland had designated as the Athenian tribe were as prominent at court as Cecil. Moreover the circle of friends was being enlarged as the men from Cambridge settled in London and began to make their way in new surroundings. The numbers were augmented as ties of mutual interest, respect, and trust developed with others who combined a love for classical studies with a Protestant persuasion. These ties of friendship in several instances were strengthened by a growing number of interlocking marriage relationships.[35]

As was true at Cambridge, it was Thomas Smith, now regius professor of civil law, who blazed the way for the advancement of others. Smith was summoned to London in February 1547, immediately after Henry VIII's death, to become Somerset's personal secre-

33. Thomas Seymour, for example, sought assiduously to win Cheke's friendship as a means of establishing an intimate relationship with the boy king. The objective was to gain Edward's affection and thus deflect the boy's loyalty from the Protector to himself as the boy king's younger uncle.

34. Read, *Mr. Secretary Cecil*, p. 76. This was partly because Northumberland was absent from court most of the time and partly because William Petre, senior principal secretary, was abroad much of the time on diplomatic missions.

35. The principal non-Cambridge "friends" of the Athenians were Anthony Cooke, Anthony Denny, Philip Hoby, Francis Knollys, Richard Morison, John Jewel, and John Parkhurst. By Elizabeth's accession, to be sure, Denny, Hoby, and Morison were dead, as was Cheke—"the chief glory of the Athenian tribe."

tary. The following month he was made both master of requests to Somerset and one of the two clerks of the Privy Council. In November he took his seat in Edward's first Parliament. In December 1547, he was elected provost of Eton, and in the following month he was appointed dean of Carlisle, the income from both posts supplementing the stipend he continued to receive as regius professor of civil law. In April 1548, Smith succeeded Paget as one of the two principal secretaries of state and was sworn to the Privy Council. In April 1549, Smith was knighted. Few could match so rapid a rise within the compass of 26 months.

Unfortunately, Smith's intellectual brilliance was not coupled with political and administrative acumen. His biographer concludes somewhat sadly that he had "little political judgment" and "no feeling for the right action at the right time." He was "incredibly insensitive," and before his career crashed in ruins with the fall of Somerset in 1549, he had alienated almost everyone by his arrogant conduct.[36] At the time he begged Petre to write him "though it be but two words of comfort."[37] He did find some comfort later, after Elizabeth's accession when Cecil used him in several important capacities until he insisted on quarreling with Cecil. By the middle of 1565 Smith had come to accept the fact that there would be for him no brilliant return to high office and that he had no friend of influence except Cecil. This recognition of his situation enabled him to escape from the limbo into which he had fallen and to reenter government service.[38]

No other member of the Cambridge group had such a meteoric rise and fall as a consequence of Edward's accession. The emergence into prominence of the other Athenians was more gradual and less dramatic. Most of those in London in 1547 were members of Edward's first Parliament, including Bacon, Cecil, Chaloner, Cheke, Richard Goodrich, Mildmay, Pickering, Thomas Smith, Throck-

36. Mary Dewar, *Sir Thomas Smith: A Tudor Intellectual in Office* (London, 1964), p. 6.
37. F. G. Emmison, *Tudor Secretary, Sir William Petre at Court and Home* (London, 1961), p. 79.
38. Dewar, *Sir Thomas Smith*, pp. 3, 81–82, 115–16. Smith used his unsought leisure to write his classic account of the English commonwealth, *De republica Anglorum*, a modern edition of which was edited by L. Alston in 1906 and published by the Cambridge University Press.

morton, and Wrothe.39 Moreover, Cooke, Mildmay, Pickering, Edward Rogers, and Wrothe were knighted at the beginning of Edward's reign. A few months later, in September, Chaloner and Francis Knollys won their spurs at the battle of Pinkie in Scotland, and Nicholas Throckmorton, who sped back to London with the news, so delighted the young king with his account of the battle that he too was knighted. Richard Sackville, as well as Smith, was knighted in 1549, Richard Morison in 1550, and Cheke and Cecil on October 11, 1551.

Of the paths pursued by the friends from Cambridge which led to their advancement in government service, demonstrated competence in financial and legal matters was the most secure. A notable example is provided by Walter Mildmay who was to become one of the great figures of Tudor financial administration. His career began in 1540 when he joined his brother as a clerk in the office of the Court of Augmentations which was charged chiefly with management of the vast monastic properties expropriated by the crown. Three years later, while continuing his work at the Court of Augmentations, he was made auditor of the king's military and naval works. In 1545 he became one of the three chief officers of the Court of General Surveyors which was charged with the administration of the older crown lands. In 1546 he was named auditor of the extensive royal properties held by the duchy of Lancaster. Also in 1546 Mildmay was the person chiefly responsible for reviewing the revenue agencies of the crown and bringing in recommendations for their reorganization.40 The principal recommendation was to merge the Court of Augmentations with the Court of General Surveyors to avoid overlapping and thus to reduce expense and permit tighter auditing and administrative controls. Although the enabling legislation for the proposed reform had not been passed at the time

39. Such intimate friends as Anthony Cooke, Anthony Denny, and Edward Rogers also were members of the 1547 Parliament. Rogers, Thomas Cranmer's brother-in-law, was linked to them by his zealous Protestantism and perhaps by congenial personality traits. Unlike others who were drawn into the Cambridge orbit, he has left little evidence of a scholarly turn of mind.

40. Also in 1546, he married Mary Walsingham, sister of Francis Walsingham and niece of Anthony Denny. For Mildmay, see S. E. Lehmberg, *Sir Walter Mildmay and Tudor Government* (Austin, Texas, 1964).

of Henry VIII's death, it was quickly enacted by Edward's newly summoned Parliament. Mildmay's contribution to the reorganization had already been recognized by the conferral of knighthood at Edward's first investiture, an extraordinary honor for a young man of twenty-seven who was neither of the royal household nor in a position to display unusual bravery and leadership on the field of battle.

Control of the reconstituted Court of Augmentations and Revenues with centralized responsibility for most of the sources of governmental revenue was vested in the chancellor, but Mildmay, as one of the two general surveyors, was in effective charge of the daily routine. At the reorganization, Richard Goodrich was transferred from his post as attorney general of the Court of Wards and Liveries to be attorney general of the new Court of Augmentations. At the same time, Nicholas Bacon was advanced from his position as solicitor general of the old Court of Augmentations to replace Goodrich as attorney general of the Court of Wards and Liveries.[41] Meanwhile Thomas Gresham, who had been apprenticed to his mercer uncle after leaving Cambridge, by 1543 was both trading for himself and acting on the king's behalf in the Low Countries. In the latter capacity he was inevitably linked to officials concerned with government revenue. Gresham became highly skilled in the management of loans and the foreign exchange rate. By late 1551 or early 1552 he had become royal agent at Antwerp and was also engaged in some diplomatic activity.[42] Gilbert Gerard who was called to the bar in 1539 was another Cambridge man at Gray's Inn during the 1530's. While apparently not holding any government posts

41. Bacon's rise was not as rapid as Mildmay's. Bacon became an "ancient" of Gray's Inn in 1536. In the middle of 1538 his name first appears on the Court of Augmentations payroll as the recipient of a meagre stipend. In September 1538 his name appears at the bottom of the annual treasurer's report of Thomas Pope. Perhaps he had helped prepare it, for he was not one of the two auditors who also signed the report. Later in 1538 he was referred to as "Mr. Solicitor." Walter Henley was the solicitor, but Bacon may have been a deputy. By 1540, however, Bacon was solicitor general of the Court of Augmentations. An indication that he was well placed to be helpful is the fact that, beginning in 1540, Cambridge University retained him intermittently, first as solicitor and eventually as attorney. For Bacon, see Robert Tittler, *Nicholas Bacon: The Making of a Tudor Statesman* (Athens, Ohio, 1976).

42. For Gresham, see J. W. Burgon, *The Life and Times of Sir Thomas Gresham* (London, 1839).

prior to the accession of Elizabeth, Gerard was building a solid reputation as a barrister and gaining sufficient respect and trust among his peers to be named treasurer of Gray's Inn.

Since the middle years of Henry VIII's reign, there had been a deliberate effort to recruit young scholars from the universities for diplomatic tasks abroad. The objective seems to have been to develop a "professional" corps of foreign service personnel and thus reduce the almost complete dependance upon ecclesiastics and merchants to serve as intermediaries in the conduct of foreign affairs and as agents for the gathering of intelligence. John Mason, William Paget, and William Petre were early examples of "the new breed" who were recruited and then sent abroad for "in-service" training and to perfect their linguistic skills. Cromwell had several men, including Richard Morison, of scholarly bent who volunteered their services. Of the younger group at Cambridge, Thomas Chaloner and William Pickering seem to have been recruited by Cromwell.[43] Both were bookish men of scholarly interests who indulged themselves in translation projects, and both were close friends of Cecil and spent most of their lives in diplomatic activity. In 1551 Pickering wrote to Cecil from his embassy in Paris that he was sending him several books, including "Euclid with the figures in a small volume." Ten days later he reported that he had found some additional books which he would forward to Cecil when they were properly bound: a Greek New Testament, notes on Aristotle's *Ethics* in Italian, and *Le Discourse de la Guerre* of Laugnay. A letter from Chaloner to Cecil, undated but probably written in 1548, provides an interesting insight into one of the guidelines Chaloner set for himself in his diplomatic contacts. After his return from Spain Chaloner was serving as clerk of the Privy Council and was sought after by resident ambassadors for tidbits of information he could provide. To Cecil he wrote: "If you have any further news which I may publish to the ambassadors here, pray write to me. I can see from this instance that in the case of evil surmise it is best to tell the tale to advantage at the beginning, for afterwards you can hardly get the first version out of their heads."[44]

43. The qualification applies to Pickering whose father was knight-marshal to Henry VIII.

44. Jordan, *Edward VI, The Young King*, p. 85. Read, *Mr. Secretary Cecil*, p. 46. Other persons involved in diplomatic activity who were closely

The royal household provided the most conspicuous opportunities for advancement. As a result of Catherine Parr's marriage to Henry VIII, her brother William became earl of Essex, and both he and Catherine's brother-in-law William Herbert received further advancement at the beginning of Edward's reign, Parr becoming marquis of Northampton and Herbert earl of Pembroke. Nicholas Throckmorton, who had been attached to the Parrs as well as having been a page to the duke of Richmond, also became a familiar figure at court after Catherine became queen, being one of the younger courtiers who clustered about the school of young Prince Edward. During Edward's reign, Throckmorton became knight of the Privy Chamber and treasurer of the Mint in the Tower.

Thomas Wrothe, a pupil of Cheke's at St. John's, illustrates the combination of circumstances which could lead to being singled out to receive honors at court. At the death of his father, who was an attorney for the duchy of Lancaster, Wrothe became a ward of Henry VIII. The wardship was transferred first to Thomas Cromwell and then to Richard Rich. Rich, who replaced Wriothesley as lord chancellor almost immediately after Edward's coronation, secured the wardship of Wrothe in order to provide a husband for his daughter. With Rich as his sponsor, Wrothe became gentleman usher to Prince Edward and then knight of the king's body and chief gentleman of his bed chamber. In spite of his early advantage and ardent Protestantism, Wrothe was never to hold a significant office. He was loyal to his friends and made himself useful in minor ways, but his role was limited primarily to that of a trusted person who could be used to round out the membership of various commissions.

CECIL DURING THE EDWARDIAN YEARS

Meanwhile where was William Cecil? According to Conyers Read, the only solid information about Cecil's life "from the time he left Gray's Inn until the death of Henry VIII" is that of his marriage to Mildred Cooke on December 21, 1545. Direct evidence concerning

---

linked to the Cambridge group were Philip and Thomas Hoby, Henry Killigrew, Richard Morison, and Nicholas Throckmorton. Also Thomas Smith was later sent on missions abroad, as were William Howard of Effingham and Francis Walsingham.

his activities in the years that followed, prior to September 5, 1550, when he was sworn to the privy council to serve with William Petre as one of the two principal secretaries of state, is still sketchy. "The indications of his activity are scant, none at all in parliamentary history and very little in administrative history."[45] Cecil's commendatory preface to Catherine Parr's *The Lamentation of a Sinner*, printed in 1547, is clear evidence, however, that Cecil had become a familiar figure of some consequence at court by the time of Henry VIII's death at the beginning of 1547.

In May 1547 Cecil entered the Protector Somerset's service. During the summer he was with the English forces in Scotland, and was present at the battle of Pinkie in September as a judge of the Marshalsea Court, the administrative instrument for enforcing discipline when troops were campaigning outside England. In October Cecil took his seat as a member of Edward's first Parliament. At the end of the year he became the Protector's personal master of requests. This was a make-shift position not related to the Court of Requests. Presumably Cecil's function was to give consideration to suits addressed to the Protector. In January, May, and June of 1548, he was utilized by Somerset in an attempt to bring Stephen Gardiner into line by inducing him to sign the visitation articles and to preach an acceptable sermon indicating his adherence to the government's religious policy. On May 6, 1548, Cecil was appointed keeper of the writs and rolls of the Common Bench. In September Cecil succeeded Thomas Fisher as Somerset's personal private secretary.

The official entries for 1549 show Cecil being named to a commission to inquire into the expropriated holdings of colleges and chantries in the city and county of Lincoln, being appointed to the office of *custos rotulorum* within the county of Lincoln, being charged by the Privy Council to assume joint responsibility with William Petre and Thomas Smith for licensing the printing of books, and named to a commission to inquire into heresies.[46] This is as far as the public record goes, but glimpses of the scope of his activities can be derived from scattered gleanings from private sources.

45. Read, *Mr. Secretary Cecil*, pp. 34, 42.
46. *Acts of the Privy Council*, ed. J. R. Dasent, New Series (London, (1890–92), II, 312. *Calendar of the Patent Rolls Preserved in the Public Record Office, Edward VI* (London, 1924–1929), II, 136, 174, 406. An entry of June 27, 1549, also shows that Cecil was accumulating extensive property holdings (ibid., pp. 354 f). See also ibid., IV, 197–99.

As Somerset's personal master of requests and private secretary, Cecil provided a major point of contact with the Protector. John Cheke approached Somerset through Cecil, and this must have been true of many others. Chaloner thought of Cecil as a primary source of information. Robert Dudley, earl of Warwick and future duke of Northumberland, regarded Cecil as a sufficiently key figure to cultivate his good will. A letter from Thomas Smith in July, written from Eton and commenting that he would soon be returning to court "to ease you from some of your pains," suggests that Cecil may have been performing tasks usually associated with the post of principal secretary of state.[47] This supposition is strengthened by the fact that the licensing of the printing of books was placed in the hands of the two principal secretaries (Petre and Smith) and Cecil.

The composition of the commission appointed April 12, 1549, to search out heretics and contemners of the prayer book provides interesting insight with regard to the persons being utilized by the government. The commission was dominated by such familiar names as Thomas Cranmer, Thomas Goodrich, Nicholas Ridley, Thomas Smith, Richard Cox, Anthony Cooke, William May, Simon Heynes, John Redman, Hugh Latimer, and William Cecil. To these names were added, in the subsequent commissions for the same purpose in 1551 and 1552, those of John Ponet, John Cheke, Rowland Taylor, Richard Goodrich, Nicholas Bacon, and Matthew Parker. From the same pool were drawn those who dominated the commissions for the visitations of the universities in 1549. The same names dominated the 1551 commission for the reform of ecclesiastical laws: Cranmer, Thomas and Richard Goodrich, Ridley, Smith, Cox, Cooke, May, Latimer, Ponet, Cheke, Rowland Taylor, Parker, and Cecil.[48] A subcommittee, composed of Ridley, Ponet, Cox, May, Rowland Taylor, Peter Martyr, and John à Lasco, was authorized to

47. Read, *Mr. Secretary Cecil*, pp. 46, 57.
48. Illustrations of the close relationships between these Athenians (or, as in the case of Cranmer and Thomas Goodrich, their sponsors) are too numerous to compile. Many instances have previously been cited. It can be noted in passing, however, that a letter from Ridley to Cecil indicates that they were "on playfully friendly terms," and that Richard Goodrich acted as Cecil's agent in the purchase of a house or houses in Cannon Row where the Thynnes, the Hobys, and the duchess of Somerset had residences. Ibid., p. 67. It may also be of some interest that after the Cambridge visitation of 1549, Cheke and his wife posted north on horseback to visit William Parr at Fotheringhay Castle.

provide an initial draft of the revised canon law. The final product, which was never given official sanction, was put into Latin by Cheke and Walter Haddon.

A common thread running through much of Cecil's activity was his involvement in religious affairs—the commissions on heresy and on the reform of ecclesiastical laws, the dealings with Stephen Gardiner, the appearance as a witness at the trials of Edmund Bonner and of Gardiner. It is not surprising, therefore, that Cecil took the lead in arranging for conferences on the Lord's Supper to be held in October and November 1551 at his home and the home of Richard Morison. The conferences were arranged in the traditional academic way as disputations with Cecil setting the rules and Cheke introducing the question. At the first conference, John Feckenham and John Young, currently imprisoned for their religious views, took the orthodox side, and were examined and confuted by David Whitehead, chaplain of the duchess of Suffolk, and Edmund Grindal and Robert Horne, both soon to be named chaplains to Edward. At the second conference, Thomas Watson, also being held for his religious views, was similarly subjected to confutation. Present as auditors at the first session were the earl of Bedford (or his son), Thomas Wrothe, Anthony Cooke, Nicholas Throckmorton, Francis Knollys, and John Harington. They were joined at the second session by William Parr, marquis of Northampton, and Henry Manners, earl of Rutland. There may have been some hope of effecting the conversion of Feckenham, Young, and Watson, but the obvious purpose was to supply the auditors with informed arguments in preparation for the forthcoming debate on the revision of the 1549 prayer book, a tactical move not dissimilar to one adopted on a more elaborate scale in a similar situation after Elizabeth's accession.

Cecil negotiated the shift of power at the end of 1549 from Somerset to the earl of Warwick without undue mishap, being confined to the Tower for only a brief period and being appointed on September 5, 1550, to serve with William Petre as principal secretary and as a member of the Privy Council. This feat was not particularly noteworthy for almost everyone survived the realignment of power, including Somerset who was readmitted to the council.49 Of greater

49. Somerset had alienated almost all his supporters. He had many faults as a political leader, being inept, imperious, and arrogant in the exercise of power. His aloofness made it difficult to work with him or for him. He

significance for the future was Cecil's agreement in the summer of 1550 at the age of 29 to act as Elizabeth's "surveyor" (supervisor of her properties and of their accounts). In accepting the responsibility, Cecil indicated that he would make use of deputies in discharging it. From hindsight, the appointment can be seen as prophetic of Cecil's relationship to Elizabeth when she became queen.

OTHER PROMOTIONS AND EJECTIONS

No account of the Cambridge connection in London would be complete without some mention of the ecclesiastics among the Athenians who also became part of the London scene. Many of the clergy who belonged to the circle of friends remained in Cambridge where, as has been noted, they dominated the university. Among the more prominent of those who continued at Cambridge were Ralph Ainsworth, Robert Beaumont, William Bill, Edmund Grindal, Edmund Guest, Roger Kelke, Thomas Lever and his brothers, James Madew, Matthew Parker, John Pedder, James Pilkington, Leonard Pilkington, Edwin Sandys, and Thomas Wilson of St. John's. Some had parish responsibilities while continuing their university connection. John Pedder, for example, remained a fellow of Peterhouse after becoming rector in 1551 at Redgrave, Suffolk, Nicholas Bacon's parish church. Others were able to serve as chaplains in this way. Still others had left the university to serve as beneficed clergy. This was true of William Alley, Edmund Scambler, and Robert Horne, the latter becoming a rector in London, chaplain to Edward VI, and then dean of Durham. William Allen left the country to study abroad but was back in England by 1549 as chaplain to Princess Elizabeth.

William May was ostensibly at Cambridge as president of Queens' College, but May collected so many posts, including that of dean of St. Paul's, and was utilized so widely for a variety of missions and commissions that he must have been more of a commuter than a

---

would not heed advice and friendly warnings. W. K. Jordan, *Edward VI: The Threshold of Power* (London, 1970), p. 106. For a reassessment of Somerset, see B. L. Beer, *Northumberland: The Political Career of John Dudley, Earl of Warwick and Duke of Northumberland* (Kent, Ohio, 1973), who indicates why Somerset has benefited from an unduly good press while Northumberland has suffered from an unduly bad press.

resident. Although they did not collect the same multiplicity of offices as William May or Stephen Gardiner, both Nicholas Ridley and John Cheke were nonresident heads of colleges. Ridley remained master of Pembroke after becoming successively bishop of Rochester and then of London. Cheke, even after becoming one of the principal secretaries of state, apparently gave no thought to resigning as provost of King's.

Richard Cox had left Cambridge for a second time when he undertook responsibility to supervise the education of young Edward, and he was almost as peripatetic as May. He too collected numerous benefices and offices. Toward the end of Edward VI's reign, however, he seems to have been giving major attention, as dean of Christ Church and chancellor of Oxford, to an endeavor, with the help of Peter Martyr as regius professor of divinity and Walter Haddon as the new master of Magdalen, to effect reform at Cambridge's sister university.

It is difficult to tell where many men were because of extensive pluralism and nonresidency. Tutors, to be sure, were apt to be closely tied to their jobs. This also was true of schoolmasters, such as Thomas Cole at the Maidstone grammar school in Kent, and Lawrence Nowell at the Sutton Coldfield grammar school in Warwickshire. Chaplains often had considerable freedom of movement, but Cranmer's chaplains seemed to have spent most of their time in residence, presumably with him in London at Lambeth. All but two of Cranmer's chaplains were Cambridge men,[50] and of the Cambridge men four of the more recent were part of the Athenian tribe—Ridley, Richard Cox, John Ponet, and Rowland Taylor. Five Athenians were to become royal chaplains to Edward VI—William Bill, Edmund Grindal, Robert Horne, Andrew Perne, and Roger Tonge.

In an earlier period, it is significant that of the seven bishops appointed in the two years after Thomas Cranmer became archbishop of Canterbury in 1533, all but one were from Cambridge. The exception was John Hilsey who was named to Rochester. Furthermore, all but one of the seven were favorers of new religious doctrines. The exception here was Rowland Lee who was appointed to Coventry and Lichfield, but it was Lee who had married Henry to

50. C. B. Rynder, "Thomas Cranmer: Ecclesiastical Patron," unpublished doctoral dissertation (University of Nebraska, 1973), p. 92.

Anne Boleyn even before Henry's own court had declared the marriage to Catherine of Aragon to be null and void.[51] This trend was moderated and then reversed after Gardiner replaced Cromwell as chief minister to the king. The situation changed once again after Henry VIII's death when Cranmer regained influence in filling episcopal vacancies as they occurred.

Of the new Edwardian appointees, those most closely identified with the Athenians were Cranmer's chaplains Nicholas Ridley and John Ponet. Ridley became bishop of Rochester in 1547 and then replaced Edmund Bonner as bishop of London in 1550. Ridley brought Edmund Grindal to London as his chaplain, and later in the same year Grindal became chaplain to the king. Ponet succeeded Ridley as bishop of Rochester in 1550 and the following year Ponet was brought to London when he took over from Gardiner as bishop of Winchester, for his principal residence then became, as it had been for Gardiner, Winchester House in Southwark. Horne almost joined Ridley and Ponet on the Episcopal Bench in 1553. Just before Edward VI's death, he was nominated but not consecrated bishop of Durham.

With the accession of Mary, the Athenian tribe was dispersed. Bishops, canons, prebends, deans, masters of colleges, regius professors, rectors of parish churches, were deprived. At first only a minimum of pressure was exerted by the government. Some of the clergy and some of the scholars at the university increasingly believed it to be expedient to make themselves as inconspicuous as possible. Some went into hiding, and some went into exile. A few conformed, and a few were martyrs. Strassburg, where Peter Martyr established his "petty college" for English theological students with the aid of John Ponet and, for a brief interlude, John Cheke, was the chief center for the exiles. The two major satellite communities were Frankfort and Zurich, with Geneva constituting a more or less isolated competing center.

Nonecclesiastics among the Athenians were similarly dispersed. Some conformed, some were imprisoned, some went into exile (more frequently perhaps to France and Italy than to the Rhine-

51. The other five were Thomas Goodrich of Ely, Edward Fox of Hereford, John Salcot of Bangor, Hugh Latimer of Worcester, and Nicholas Shaxton of Salisbury. The latter two, appointed in 1535, resigned their bishoprics in 1539.

land). There were some seemingly who were not put to the test. Most often these were bureaucrats who lived quietly and whose technical skills made them indispensable. A few made a distinction between active support of the queen and legal acceptance of her authority. This seems to have been the view of William Cecil who withdrew almost completely from public life. He was willing to submit to an outward conformity and to serve the commonweal as a private man but not as an official counsellor and participant in the new government.

VI. THE RELIGIOUS SETTLEMENT OF 1559: ATHENIAN INVOLVEMENT

When the Spanish ambassador discovered on November 10, 1558, that Mary Tudor was dying, he hurriedly sought out Elizabeth to ascertain her intentions. Four days later he reported the impression he had gained in a dispatch to Philip of Spain. "I greatly fear that in religion she will not go right, as I perceive she is inclined to govern by men who are held to be heretics. And they tell me that the ladies who are most about her are all so. Besides this, she shows herself highly indignant at the things done to her in the lifetime of the queen."[1] Seven days after the interview Mary was dead and Elizabeth was queen.

In spite of the clues provided by the Spanish ambassador's assessment of Elizabeth's intentions, few topics have been the subject of more debate than the Elizabethan religious settlement of 1559. One reason for this is that the absence of clearcut evidence at certain points in official documents[2] has left room for considerable speculation. The task of untangling the course of events and unraveling the interplay of influences shaping the settlement has been further complicated by the tendency of Elizabeth and Cecil to be less than forthright in disclosing their intentions. Cecil, with few exceptions, tended to keep his own counsel, and he seldom showed his hand when engaged in a delicate political operation. Elizabeth, for her part, compounded the problem for the historian by statements which seem to have been deliberately designed to be misleading.

By the time she became queen, she had become skilled in the art of dissimulation—dissimulation designed not only to hide but to mislead. This had been the price of her survival. Sometimes her evasive and ambiguous responses to questions verged on outright

1. P. F. Tytler, ed., *England under the Reigns of Edward VI and Mary* (London, 1839), II, 495 ff.
2. Records of the Privy Council and reports of parliamentary proceedings, for example, are often sketchy, lacking in detail, and sometimes missing.

deceit, or so it seemed to some members of the diplomatic corps resident in London. "Until now," a communication of December 31, 1558, in the Venetian papers states, "I have believed that matters of religion would continue in the accustomed manner, her Majesty having promised this with her own mouth many times." He must have been unusually ill-informed and guilty of wishful thinking to have accepted Elizabeth's reassurances that the Marian legislation would remain intact. Even after the adoption of the Act of Uniformity attempts at dissimulation continued, but skepticism replaced the former trust. "The queen would still wish to some extent to feign to profess the Catholic religion but she can conceal herself no longer."[3] By July 27, 1559, the bishop of Aquila, writing of Elizabeth from London to Philip of Spain, expressed his own disenchantmen: "I have lost all hope in the affairs of this woman. . . . In religious matters she has been saturated ever since she was born in a bitter hatred of our faith, and her one object is to destroy it. . . . Besides this her language (learnt from Italian friars who brought her up) is so shifty that it is the most difficult thing to negotiate with her."[4]

Sometimes the fault in finding ambiguity in Elizabeth's language has been not with Elizabeth but with subsequent historians who have wrested her words from their context and given them a meaning quite contrary to what she intended. A notable example of such perverse misinterpretation relates to the Spanish ambassador's report of Elizabeth's comment that she was "resolved to restore religion as her father left it," a comment utilized to assert that Elizabeth intended a return to the Henrician religious legislation. Since she had already objected to the elevation of the host in the royal chapel and was ready, by anyone's interpretation of the evidence, to accept communion in both kinds, a return to Henrician legislation obviously was not what she had in mind. If one notes the date of the letter, March 19, 1559, and the ambassador's comment that he found Elizabeth "resolved about what was yesterday passed in Parliament" (the Act of Supremacy), it is clear that Elizabeth meant no more than

3. *Calendar of State Papers, Venetian, 1558–70,* VII, 2, 81.
4. *Calendar of State Papers, Spanish, 1558–67,* I, 89. Elizabeth later acknowledged quite explicitly to the Spanish ambassador, perhaps in a further effort at dissimulation, that on occasion she had had to conceal her real feelings in matters of religion. Ibid. p. 387.

that it was her intention to do as her father had done and keep religion firmly under the control of the crown, a prerogative she consistently and emotionally defended throughout her life.

Elizabeth was unusually blunt and forthright in this interview. She was excited and elated by news that peace had been concluded with France. Count de Feria's report was clear and unambiguous.

> I found her resolved about what yesterday passed in Parliament, and which Cecil and vice-chamberlain Knollys and their followers have managed to bring about for their own ends. She said after a time that she could not marry your Majesty as she was a heretic. I was much surprised to hear her use such words and begged her to tell me the cause of so great a change since I last discussed the subject with her. . . . She kept repeating that she was heretical and consequently could not marry your Majesty. She was so disturbed and excited and resolved to restore religion as her father left it, that at last I said that I did not consider she was heretical and could not believe that she would sanction the things which were being discussed in Parliament. She said that she would not take the title head of the church but that so much money was taken out of the country for the pope each year that she must put an end to it, and that the bishops were lazy poltroons. I replied that the poltroons were the preachers she listened to and that it added little to her honor and was a great scandal that so many rogues would come from Germany and get into the pulpit before her and great congregations to preach a thousand absurdities without being learned or worthy to be listened to.[5]

What better account of Elizabeth, in an unguarded moment, could one wish?

Actually, in spite of not knowing everything one might wish to know about the Elizabethan religious settlement, there is much solid evidence which need not be twisted to provide a coherent and consistent understanding of the settlement. Moreover, the shaping of the Elizabethan settlement, when placed within the context of those who played key roles in effecting it, is far from being as puzzling and complex as it has sometimes been made to appear.

Much can be said with reasonable assurance about the Elizabethan

5. Ibid., pp. 37–38.

religious settlement. Before examining in detail the process by which the settlement was reached, there are two preliminary conclusions which need not be susceptible of great debate.

Conyers Read stated the first conclusion with his comment that "the Anglican [religious] establishment in all its essential particulars was clearly defined in the last years of Edward's reign."[6] By this statement, Read meant that the twin pillars of the Elizabethan religious settlement were the reaffirmation of the royal supremacy and the adoption of the 1552 Edwardian prayer book as the basis for religious uniformity.

The Act of Supremacy is quite straightforward in reaffirming the royal supremacy with a single happy alteration. To the satisfaction of everyone, the title "supreme governor" of the church replaced the Henrician term "supreme head" of the church.[7] Although John Parkhurst commented that the change in title amounted to the same thing, the main objection to the Henrician terminology was based on the theological ground that Christ alone is the "head" of the church. John Jewel reported that Elizabeth shared the opinion that "this honor is due to Christ alone."[8]

The Act of Uniformity is equally straightforward in making it clear that the second Edwardian prayer book was being restored. The Act of Uniformity, which served as a preface to the 1559 prayer book, stated:

> Whereas at the death of our late sovereign lord, King Edward
> VI, there remained one uniform order of common service and

6. *Mr. Secretary Cecil and Queen Elizabeth* (New York, 1961), p. 83. Read continues: "All that Elizabeth and her theologians did later was to modify it a little here and there, to explain it, and to justify it. She did not create it." Ibid.

7. Edwin Sandys wrote to Matthew Parker, April 30, 1559, explaining the change: "Mr. Lever wisely put such a scruple in the queen's head that she would not take the title of supreme head." *Correspondence of Matthew Parker* (Cambridge, 1853), p. 66.

8. *Zurich letters, 1558–1579* (Cambridge, 1842), pp. 29, 33. Elizabeth's earlier resistance to the change had been stiffened by Roman Catholic insistence voiced by Archbishop Heath that only a man could represent Christ as head of the church. When given an alternative reason to make the change in terminology, Elizabeth abandoned her resistance.

prayer ... in the Church of England ... authorized by Act of Parliament holden in the fifth and sixth years of our said late sovereign ..., the which was repealed and taken away by Act of Parliament in the first year of our late sovereign lady, Queen Mary, to the great decay of the true honor of God and discomfort to the professors of the truth of Christ's religion:

Be it therefore enacted ... that the said statute of repeal and everything therein contained ... shall be void and of none effect from and after the feast of the nativity of St. John Baptist, next coming. And that the said book ..., with the alteration and additions ... appointed by this statute shall stand and be ... in full force and effect.

And be it further enacted ... that all and singular ministers ... within this realm ... shall ... be bounden to say and use the said book, so authorized by Parliament in the said fifth and sixth year of the reign of King Edward VI, with one alteration or addition of certain lessons ..., and the form of the Litany altered and corrected, and two sentences only added in the delivery of the Sacrament to the communicants, and none other or otherwise.9

There is no hint that the 1549 book was considered to serve as the basis for religious uniformity in 1559, and all contemporary references take it for granted that it was the 1552 book that was being restored.10

Elizabeth is often supposed to have favored the 1549 book, but no convincing evidence has been adduced to support this supposition. J. E. Neale, who mistakenly believed Elizabeth to have been thwarted in her desire to restore the Henrician religious legislation, concluded that she must have preferred as second-best a return to the 1549 book. He then by sleight of hand equated the 1549 book with the Augsburg Confession to bolster his conclusion, and finally called attention to "that preference in high quarters for the first Edwardian book, which is so evident in Guest's apologetic letter." John Jewel, on the other hand, speaking for those seeking the

9. *The Prayer Book of Queen Elizabeth, 1559 ..., the Whole Printed from the Originals in the British Museum* (London, 1890).

10. *Zurich Letters, 1558–1579*, pp. 28, 29, 33; *Zurich Letters, 1558–1602*, Second series (Cambridge, 1845), pp. 19, 161; *Correspondence of Matthew Parker*, pp. 65, 66.

restoration of the 1552 book, reported that Elizabeth "openly favors our cause," is "earnest in the cause of true religion," "desires a thorough change as early as possible," and "is favorably and propitiously disposed towards us." If this was Jewel's opinion, how could Edmund Guest, his friend and colleague, have thought otherwise? They were engaged in common enterprises at the time. Cecil also was reported to have been "earnest" in his support of the 1552 book.[11]

Confusion at this point was created when John Strype mistakenly assumed that an undated letter attributed to Edmund Guest belonged to the period immediately prior to the adoption of the Elizabethan Act of Uniformity. Cecil had come upon the letter inadvertently

11. Neale, "The Elizabethan Acts of Supremacy and Uniformity," *English Historical Review*, LXV (1950): 328 *Zurich Letters, 1558–1579*, pp. 10, 18, 33; *Correspondence of Matthew Parker*, p. 65. Neale's sleight-of-hand is based on two items. The first is a grumpy letter from Richard Hilles to Bullinger on February 28, 1559, in which he takes issue with Bullinger, indicates his own preference for the Confession of Augsburg, and states that there is "a general expectation that all rites and ceremonies will shortly be reformed by our faithful citizens and other godly men in the aforementioned Parliament either after the pattern which was lately in use in the time of King Edward the Sixth or which is set forth by the Protestant princes of Germany in the above-named Confession of Augsburg." *Zurich Letters, 1558–1602*, Second series, pp. 14–17. The wish must have been father to the thought, for there is no indication that the latter possibility was seriously entertained in Parliament. The other item is a report by Count de Feria, the Spanish ambassador, of an interview with Elizabeth on April 29, the day the uniformity bill passed the Lords. In a rather stumbling, incoherent way, as though she were not sure of her ground, Elizabeth told him that "she wished the Augustanean confession to be maintained in her realm." Then she added: "It would not be the Augustanean confession but something else like it." This "phrase," Neale contends, "we may take to correspond to the 1549 prayer book." Neale, *English Historical Review*, LXV (1950), 318, and Neale, *Elizabeth I and Her Parliaments* (London, 1953), p. 79. This is a strange interpretation, for even at this late date, had Elizabeth wished to tell the ambassador that she favored the 1549 prayer book, there is no reason why she should not have said so. Diplomatic negotiations, however, were being carried on with the German princes at the time, and this easily could have been an attempt at a subtle reminder that the English were not left without friends. At best this would have been a rather confused diplomatic ploy, but it makes more sense than to suggest that she really meant to indicate her preference for the 1549 prayer book by referring to the Augsburg Confession. Moreover, what else than a diplomatic ploy could Elizabeth have had in mind on the very day that the bill establishing the 1552 prayer book had passed the second of the two Houses of Parliament, a bill that she was prepared to sign and did sign?

when, at Matthew Parker's request, he was looking for something else. Unable to find the item Parker wanted, Cecil sent him Guest's letter, thinking it might be of some interest to the archbishop as an item to be included in the manuscript collections he was assembling. The letter, addressed only to "Right honorable," was unsolicited, and Guest excused himself for being "so bold to write your honor some causes of the order taken in the new service," expressing the hope that "you will take it well for my good meaning." [12] The letter clearly is not addressed to the issues of 1559 since four of the suggestions Guest earnestly puts forward had been incorporated in the 1552 book. The letter belongs to the period just prior to the adoption of the 1552 book when the council was actively canvassing the changes to be made in the 1549 book. A major portion of the letter is devoted to the question of kneeling, which was a key issue in 1552 but not in 1559. [13] The "right honorable" to whom the letter was addressed was probably Cecil for the letter was in his files, and it would have been appropriate in 1552 to address such a letter to him as a principal secretary of the council.

12. The letter is printed in Henry Gee, *The Elizabethan Prayer-Book and Ornaments* (London, 1902); and in H. G. Dugdale, *The Life and Character of Edmund Geste* (London, 1940).

13. Cranmer reported that the issue of kneeling had been well-weighed at the making of the 1552 book. See his letter printed in Gee, *The Elizabethan Prayer-Book*, p. 225. Few have given much attention to Gee's contentions that Guest's letter can only have been written in connection with the 1552 book, and one writer has so given rein to his imagination that he suggests that the letter was written in response to a request by Elizabeth. It is equally farfetched to identify the letter with a statement by Sandys on April 30, 1559. Sandys was discussing the attempt by some Roman Catholics to persuade Elizabeth to veto the final Act of Uniformity on the basis that "in the time of consecration we give no thanks." Sandys then comments that "we have ministered reasons to maintain that part." *Correspondence of Matthew Parker*, p. 66. While the Guest letter does deal with this issue, it raises too many other issues at this late date to be "the reasons" Sandys says they have submitted to Elizabeth to counter an objection that had been raised as a last ditch effort to persuade her to withhold her assent. With Guest's letter so clearly addressed to the issues of 1552 and in the absence of any solid evidence that in 1559 a return to the 1549 book was being seriously considered, it would seem perverse to supply the lack of evidence at this point by positing a consideration of the 1549 book in 1559 on the basis of a letter which fits neatly only into the discussions being carried on in 1552. The constant reference in Guest's letter to the "first book" without any mention of the "second book" should be sufficient evidence in itself that the letter belongs to 1552 and not to 1559.

The remarkable feature of the 1559 prayer book, following its adoption in April, is that the few changes from the 1552 book evoked little discussion and occasioned no significant dissent, other than Roman Catholic opposition to the book as a whole.[14] The shifts that were made in the lessons and a number of minor verbal alterations were of no theological significance. There was no apparent disagreement about omitting from the Litany, as unnecessarily offensive, the petition for deliverance from "the tyranny of the bishop of Rome and all his detestable enormities." Nor was there any apparent debate about adding two sentences from the 1549 book to the 1552 wording for the giving of the bread and the cup to the communicants, so that the amended formulas read as follows with the 1549 insertions italicized:

> *The body of our lord Jesus Christ, which was given for thee, preserve thy body and soul into everlasting life:* And take and eat this in remembrance that Christ died for thee, feed on him in thine heart by faith with thanksgiving.

> *The blood of our lord Jesus Christ, which was shed for thee, preserve thy body and soul into everlasting life:* And drink this in remembrance that Christ's blood was shed for thee and be thankful.

No one could really object to the inclusion of the biblical phrases, but a changed situation explains the general agreement that the additional wording was desirable.

In 1552 the major concern had been to make clear the rejection of any notion of transubstantiation. By 1559 this was no longer a problem. The issue had been settled in dramatic fashion in December 1558 by Elizabeth when she refused to countenance the elevation of the host and walked out of the royal chapel as a mark of her displeasure and to indicate her rejection of the doctrine of transubstantiation.

14. C. W. Dugmore commented that J. E. Neale was guilty of at least exaggeration when he stated that "by November 1558, so far as the *émigrés* were concerned, the second Edwardian prayer book had ceased to be 'most godly,'" (*The Mass and the English Reformers* [London, 1958], p. 209). This was true no doubt of the exiles at Geneva, but Neale ignores the existence of the "powerful prayer book party" among the exiles elsewhere. The Genevans returned late to England and played no significant role in the Elizabethan settlement.

If the issue of transubstantiation had been settled for the English church by 1559, the one thing the major figures involved in the Elizabethan settlement would wish to make clear was their belief in a real presence and their conviction that the sacrament was no mere memorial. Martin Bucer and Peter Martyr had been their tutors at this point, and, as a result of intramural discussion among Protestants, both Calvin and Bullinger would have agreed upon a real presence of Christ in the sacrament to those who fed on him in faith. Jewel assured Peter Martyr on April 28, 1559, that we "have not departed in the slightest degree from the confession of Zurich."[15] Although he was referring to some "articles of religion and doctrine" that had been drafted for the queen, this was the day on which the 1559 prayer book had received its final approval. Jewel would scarcely have assured Martyr of entire agreement with Zurich on this specific date had he not believed that the prayer book also was in harmony with the Zurich confession, pressumably because the wording for the administration of the sacrament had been clarified.[16]

These then were the twin pillars of the Elizabethan religious settlement—the royal supremacy and the 1552 Edwardian prayer book. Of the twin pillars, there are hints of some qualms about the first, the Act of Supremacy, which the shift in terminology from "supreme head" to "supreme governor" of the Church of England did not fully allay. Given the exigency of the time, however, these qualms were muted. With regard to the second pillar, the point of unease and disquiet to those promoting the settlement was not the prayer book itself. This appears to have been generally acceptable. What was worrisome to those who were not privy to what we may presume to have been Cecil's strategy, and which was utilized in an unforeseen way to provoke dissention in the future, was a "proviso" in the Act of Uniformity postponing for the present any decision with regard to the use of "ornaments." The issue was left to be determined "by the authority of the Queen's Majesty with the advice

15. *Zurich Letters, 1558–1579*, pp. 19–20.
16. The so-called black rubric added by Edward VI, which bluntly stated that kneeling was not an act of adoration implying a belief in transubstantiation, had not received parliamentary approval and technically was not a part of the 1552 prayer book. In 1559 it was allowed to disappear without debate. The changed theological climate obviated the necessity for such a disclaimer. Neither queen, Privy council, Parliament, nor clerical leaders seem to have given any thought to retaining the rubric.

of her commissioners appointed . . . for causes ecclesiastical or of the metropolitan of this realm." Until then, "such ornaments of the church and of the ministers thereof shall be retained and be in use as was in this Church of England by authority of Parliament in the second year of the reign of King Edward VI."

PROTESTANT INVOLVEMENT IN THE SETTLEMENT

The second conclusion which should not be susceptible of great debate is that the key figures in the new regime, both in governmental and ecclesiastical affairs, were Protestants by conviction and were linked to one another by intimate ties of friendship. The Spanish ambassador, reporting on his interview with Elizabeth seven days before Mary's death, was remarkably accurate in his appraisal that Elizabeth intended to "govern by men" who were generally esteemed to be "heretics." Chief among them was William Cecil who he believed would be her principal secretary. The others whom Elizabeth chose were, for the most part, Cecil's friends. They were part of the network of relationships which first took shape at Cambridge and was somewhat enlarged as kindred spirits in London were drawn within the Athenian orbit.

Most of the patrons of the Athenian tribe—Dr. William Butts, Catherine Parr, Anthony Denny, Thomas Cranmer—were dead, as was John Cheke, around whose personality the group had first coalesced. Ridley, like Cranmer and Latimer, had suffered martyrdom. John Ponet, James Haddon, and Richard Morison had died in exile. But others remained to assume posts in the government. Among them were Nicholas Bacon, Walter Mildmay (who later founded Emmanuel College to be a seedplot of godly preachers), Francis Russell, William Parr, and Francis Knollys. All were earnest Protestants. And there were others in the government who were equally dependable as allies and friends.

While it is true, as J. E. Neale observed, that at the beginning of her reign "Elizabeth must have listened to a babel of conflicting advice" with regard to religious policy,[17] the important question is to whom did she pay attention, whose advice did she heed? On July 15, 1561, Cecil wrote Nicholas Throckmorton that the Spanish

17. "The Elizabethan Acts of Supremacy and Uniformity," *English Historical Review* LXV (1950): 307.

ambassador was accusing him of being the author of the religious changes that had been made, and Cecil commented: "I must confess that I am thereof guilty but not thereby at fault, and thereto I will stand as long as I shall live." [18] At a later date Cecil wrote Edward Dering how active he had been "above all others in propagating religion in the beginning of the queen," undergoing "many and great labors in anxieties and disquiets of mind," and "enduring great contestation in it." Still later, in 1574, Thomas Sampson reminded Cecil of what his role had been in the alteration of religion: "What your authority, credit, and doing then was; you know, God knows, and there are witnesses to it." [19] In the absence of evidence to the contrary, there is little reason to question Cecil's claim that, in collaboration with others, he was the chief architect of the Elizabethan religious settlement, and thus to conclude that it was primarily Cecil to whom Elizabeth listened and whose advice, with perhaps two or three exceptions, she heeded. Still Elizabeth's general attitude on religious issues always had to be taken into account in order to secure her assent for specific policies. One may suppose that this latter necessity made the settlement less tidy than Cecil may have wished or even intended.

Cecil's claim is plausible for several reasons. Elizabeth had singled out Cecil as her confidant, trusted advisor, and chief minister during the session at Hatfield House immediately after Mary's death. Indeed, Cecil had been active in drafting plans and getting things done for at least ten days prior to Elizabeth's dramatic charge to him on November 20. Even before Elizabeth's accession the central role Cecil was to play was apparent both to the Spanish ambassador and to Nicholas Heath, Mary's lord chancellor. After the event, the Spanish ambassador found confirmation of his earlier judgment. On December 14, 1558, he described Cecil as "the man who does everything." On March 19, 1559, he was convinced that Cecil "governs the queen." [20] As a result of her affair with Dudley, in the late summer and early fall of 1560 Elizabeth did waver in her reliance

18. Conyers Read, *Mr. Secretary Cecil*, p. 128. This was not a new charge. As early as January 31, 1559, writing of the religious situation, the Spanish ambassador asserted: "The members of the council who are foremost in upsetting things are Cecil and the earl of Bedford [Francis Russell]." *C.S.P., Spanish, 1558–67*, I, 25.

19. John Strype, *Annals of the Reformation* (Oxford, 1824), I, i, 119, 120.

20. *C.S.P., Spanish, 1558–67*, I, 10, 38.

upon Cecil, but this was after the religious settlement had been effected.

Cecil's claim is plausible also because as a convinced Protestant he had a personal stake in the religious settlement. There is ample evidence to support the verdict of Philip Hughes that Cecil "was a very sincere, pious, and wholehearted Protestant."[21] One might add that he was well informed and knowledgeable, as well as pious, in matters of religion. This, one may suppose, is the reason why he was used in such matters under Edward, for involvement in religious affairs was a common thread running through many of the assignments given him by Somerset and Northumberland.

The most convincing evidence of Cecil's hand in fashioning and directing the strategy and tactics for resolving the religious issue at the outset of Elizabeth's reign is that, almost to a man, all the clergy utilized in the project fell within the orbit of Cecil's friends. This is particularly telling evidence since the recruiting of clerical personnel for specific tasks, in the absence of a metropolitan, would be a normal responsibility of the principal secretary, and it became an official responsibility when members of the Privy Council were constituted "commissioners" for "causes ecclesiastical."

Those whose names recur repeatedly in the assignments that were made to forward a religious settlement numbered no more than nine or ten. Some had gone into exile, some had not. Most were both university men and churchmen. They were devout Protestants, earnest reformers, and even those who occupied university posts tended to be devoted to preaching and pastoral care. They were heirs of a common Cambridge Protestant tradition. Of those who went into exile under Mary, most were at Strassburg and from there they intervened in the dispute at Frankfort in a successful defense of the 1552 prayer book. If one wished to hazard a guess with regard to the theological orientation of Cecil's personal piety, one would

21. *The Reformation in England* (London, 1954), III, 4. Cecil's letters of comfort and consolation to friends who were sick or bereaved should provide sufficient support for Hughes' verdict. Cecil's directions for his son Thomas reveal his deep religious convictions, being almost entirely concerned with his son's spiritual welfare. Conyers Read, referring to these "directions," commented that they exhibit "the strong Puritan strain" in Cecil and represent a sermon he preached many times. *Mr. Secretary Cecil*, pp. 213–14. It is also significant that one of Cecil's chief preoccupations with his wards was to inculcate in them a firm Protestant piety.

assume that it would bear some correlation to that of his friends who were closely related to and influenced by Martin Bucer and his friend and colleague Peter Martyr.[22] Whether or not this is true, it is clear that Cecil did rely on his friends to help effect the religious settlement in 1559.

The clergy most intimately involved in the activity which prepared the way for the settlement were, with only two exceptions, Cambridge men. Three of them had been at St. John's with Cecil. The latter were *William Bill*, ejected master of Trinity College; *Robert Horne*, ejected fellow of St. John's; and *Edwin Sandys*, ejected master of St. Catherine's. The others from Cambridge were *Richard Cox, Edmund Grindal, Matthew Parker*,[23] and *William May*. The two exceptions were *David Whitehead*[24] and *John Jewel*.[25] One other name perhaps should be added to the list, although he really did not belong to the inner circle. This was *Thomas Sampson* whose connection at Cambridge was with Pembroke College. Sampson was utilized for a time, chiefly to take advantage of his eloquence as a preacher. He proved to be a disappointment, anguishing over what seemed to others to be petty quibbles. Bullinger had discovered this unhappy characteristic of Sampson when he was in Zurich. Bullinger wrote to Beza in Geneva that he "always looked with suspicion on statements made by Master Sampson," and then made the further comment about Sampson: "While

22. For a discussion of this point, see J. C. McLelland, "Calvinism Perfecting Thomism? Peter Martyr Vermigli's Question," *Scottish Journal of Theology* XXXI (1978): 576–77. See also W. M. Southgate's early essay, "The Marian Exiles and the Influence of John Calvin," *History* XXVII (1942): 148–52.

23. Parker was not as directly involved for he remained in Cambridge and was in London only intermittently to preach at Paul's Cross, to preach a Lenten sermon before the queen, and to confer with his friends. Sandys lamented his absence, writing on April 30, 1559: "I wish we had your hand" in drawing up for the queen "the sum of that doctrine which we profess. . . . Ye cannot long rest in your cell. Ye must be removed to a more large abbey." *Correspondence of Matthew Parker*, p. 66.

24. Reputedly educated at Oxford, Whitehead was a highly respected figure at court under Edward VI. He had been a Protestant spokesman, with Grindal and Horne, at the disputations held in the homes of Richard Morison and William Cecil in 1551. He had declined Cranmer's recommendation that he be named archbishop of Armagh.

25. Jewel had been at Strassburg and then had followed Peter Martyr to Zurich. Although a graduate of Oxford, he always included himself among the Cambridge "Athenians" when he spoke of "our friends."

he resided amongst us at Zurich and after he returned to England, he never ceased to be troublesome to Master Peter Martyr. . . . He often used to complain to me that Sampson never wrote a letter without filling it with grievances. The man is never satisfied. He always has some doubt or other to busy himself with. . . . I certainly have a natural dislike to men of this stamp."[26]

William Bill appeared first on the scene, summoned from his place of retirement at Sandy, Bedfordshire, to preach at Paul's Cross on the day Elizabeth's council met for the first time at Hatfield. Cecil's concern was to secure a reliable person who would not use the occasion to stir up "any dispute concerning the governance of the realm," and Bill was his choice. The following Sunday the bishop of Chichester preached a bitter rejoinder, and was immediately called before the queen and remanded to be confined. All preaching was then suspended until February 10, 1559, when the Paul's Cross sermons were reinstituted with Matthew Parker as the initial preacher. Subsequent preachers at the Cross were Grindal, Horne, Sandys, Jewel, and Thomas Bentham.[27] Preachers of the Lenten sermons before the queen were Parker, Grindal, Sandys, Cox, and Whitehead. The related 'Spital sermons before Easter were given by Bill, Cox, and Horne, with Sampson delivering the "rehearsal sermon" at Paul's Cross. The latter sermons were related to the Easter recess of Parliament, during which period a disputation was held at Westminster as an endeavor to discredit the Marian bishops and thus reduce their influence in the upper house of Parliament. The Protestant participants in the disputation were Grindal, Sandys, Cox, Horne, Jewel, Whitehead, John Scory, and Edmund Guest.[28] Cox preached the sermon at the opening of Parliament, reminding the members of their duty. When the 1559 prayer book was brought into use in June 1559, Grindal was called upon to proclaim and explain at Paul's Cross the restoration of "King Edward's Book."

The two chief clerical representatives on the nineteen-member Ecclesiastical Commission, appointed July 19, 1559, were Parker

26. Dugmore, *The Mass and the English Reformers*, pp. 223–24.

27. Bentham was an Oxford graduate who was in exile at Zurich before returning to England to preach privately to Protestants in London.

28. Aylmer and Guest are familiar as members of the Athenian tribe at Cambridge. Scory was of the preceding generation at Cambridge, a Dominican friar who became an Edwardian bishop, was deprived under Mary and went into exile.

and Grindal. They belonged to the commission's inner committee of six. The other two clerical members were William Bill and William May, and then in October Richard Cox was added. Prior to the appointment of the commission, committees of laymen had been named to carry out ecclesiastical visitations in the several parts of the kingdom. One or two preachers were included in each committee to interpret the proceedings: Sandys was named for the visitation of the North, Horne for London and East Anglia, Alexander Nowell and Thomas Becon for the South and Southeast, Jewel for the Southwest, Alexander Nowell and Thomas Bentham for the Midlands, and Richard Davies and Thomas Young for Wales. Eton and Cambridge were set apart to be visited by a group hand-picked for the purpose: Cecil, Walter Haddon, Thomas Wendy (physician to the queen), and others whose names are so familiar: Matthew Parker, William Bill, William May, Robert Horne, and James Pilkington.

Further confirmation of the pervasive role of this small group of clergy are the initial episcopal appointments. As pointed out earlier, Scory and Barlow were Cambridge men but, as Edwardian bishops, they may be disregarded. They represented no free choice of the new regime. The policy of appointing Welshmen to posts in Wales also places them in a separate category. With these exceptions, the initial appointments were: Matthew Parker, consecrated archbishop of Canterbury, December 20, 1559; Edmund Grindal (London); Richard Cox (Ely); and Edwin Sandys (Worcester) all consecrated on December 21, 1559.[29] Within a week thereafter, the appointment of Jewel to Salisbury received the assent of the queen. Appointments to the northern province were delayed, but the initial nominee for archbishop of York was William May who died before he could be elected and consecrated.

Three of the ten who have been identified as being most intimately involved in the religious settlement did not become bishops. William Bill may have been happy to serve as a bridge between Cambridge and London with his triple appointments, or perhaps he was in ill

29. If he had not died in the interim, Edmund Allen, a contemporary of Cecil's at Cambridge, would have been consecrated bishop of Rochester at this time. Allen, elected a fellow of Corpus Christi in 1536 and steward in 1539, was an exile whom Elizabeth made one of her royal chaplains on his return. He was nominated and elected to the see of Rochester under a *congé d'élire* dated July 27, 1559.

health for he died in 1561. David Whitehead, at an advanced age, declined all appointments, saying that he was delighted to travel "to and fro" to preach the word of God where he felt it was needed. Sampson was considered for an episcopal seat but it is not clear whether an offer was ultimately withheld or declined. Robert Horne, the last of the clerics who had been most conspicuous in the activity surrounding the settlement, had been reinstated as dean of Durham but a variety of circumstances delayed his advancement until February 1561 when he became bishop of Winchester.

Appointments to the other sees followed much the same pattern as the early consecrations. Most were Cambridge men. Three were Oxford graduates, John Parkhurst, Thomas Bentham, and Nicholas Bullingham, who were linked to the Cambridge Athenian group. Most were university professionals rather than men who had pursued ecclesiastical preferment as a path to advancement. A majority had been exiles under Mary, primarily at Strassburg, Zurich, and Frankfort. Those of the bishops who had not gone into exile had lived in hiding or obscurity. One had traveled about practicing medicine, and two had preached to secret Protestant congregations. The only exception was William Downham, bishop of Chester, who had served as Elizabeth's chaplain under Queen Mary.[30]

It is difficult to believe that these bishops were random choices determined by the luck of the draw. For one thing, many of them fell within the category of Cecil's friends. Moreover, they included almost all those who had been utilized repeatedly in various capacities at the outset of the reign. Furthermore, there is compelling evidence that Cecil had a hand in their selection, keeping in mind always that all suggestions for vacant sees had to be confirmed by the queen.[31]

30. Other bishops educated at Cambridge were James Pilkington, a contemporary of Cecil at St. John's; Edmund Guest, also a Cambridge contemporary of Cecil; Edmund Scambler, another Cambridge contemporary of Cecil; William Alley, who antedated Cecil at Cambridge but was a contemporary of John Cheke; and Richard Cheyney, who had supported Cheke's advocacy of the Erasmian prounciation of Greek.

31. Patrick Collinson speaks of "the ecclesiastical influence" Robert Dudley "exercised from the beginning of Elizabeth's reign," and suggests that "of the first generation of Elizabethan bishops, at least six . . . seem to have owed their preferment at least partly to his influence" (*Letters of Thomas Wood, Puritan, 1566–1577*, Bulletin of the Institute of Historical Research, Special Supplement No. 5 [University of London, 1960], pp. xxi–xxii). This

The lengthy correspondence seeking to induce a reluctant Matthew Parker to accept the responsibilities of the archbishop of Canterbury reveal Cecil and Bacon working hand in glove to accomplish this purpose. In the exchange of letters both Bacon and Parker make it clear that Bacon was acting as his brother-in-law's agent. Bacon's first letter to Parker speaks of "certain matters" which shall "turn you to good" and requests Parker to come to London as soon as possible. If he did not find Bacon in the city, Parker should repair to Cecil "to know *his* pleasure touching such matters as he and I did talk of concerning you." Parker, in his response, makes it equally plain that he regarded Cecil, "of long time my special good friend and master," as the one who had taken the initiative, for Parker asks Bacon to persuade Cecil to desist from "*his* mediation to do me good." Parker then adds concerning Cecil: "I would be inwardly heavy and sorry that *his* favorable affection should procure me anything above the reach of my ability." On the following page Parker

---

conclusion, with one exception, is based on inferences drawn from post-1565 materials and relationships. It is worth noting that three of the six—Sandys, Horne, and Pilkington—were close friends of Cecil and had been fellow students with him at St. John's, and that two of the remaining three—Grindal and Scambler—had been Cecil's contemporaries at Cambridge. Dudley's preoccupation with ecclesiastical appointments is generally considered to have followed the failure in 1561 of his intrigue with the Spanish ambassador and with some of the Roman Catholic gentry to forward his marriage prospects with Elizabeth. It is true, of course, that people sought patronage and support wherever they could find it, and "the favorite" was a person whose aid would be welcomed and cultivated. It is not surprising, therefore, that Sandys should have written Dudley on April 14, 1560: "I thank you for commending me to your friends . . . and pray you to maintain my honest and right cause as hitherto ye have done." This cryptic comment, however, is scarcely sufficient to attribute to Dudley Sandys' nomination to the episcopal bench. Dudley's commendation probably was related to a lengthy dispute between Sandys and Parker to which Sandys refers in a letter of October 24, 1560. Parker, in several long letters had accused Sandys of using his power of "visitation" for "private gain" before he was even "lukewarm in his place," of stirring up anti-Parker sentiment, of sending his letters to Parker to be reviewed by Grindal before they were forwarded to Parker, and of seeking "a favor [perhaps from Dudley] against another day." The whole business as set forth in the letter is very murky, and Sandys complains of Parker's "dark sentences" which he found difficult to understand and interpret. The letter, however, makes it clear that Sandys in the early spring and summer of 1560 stood in need of someone who would help him "maintain" his "honest and right cause." *Correspondence of Matthew Parker*, pp. 124–27.

again implores Bacon to convey his wish to be excused to "Mr. Secretary." On December 30, 1558, Cecil writes directly to Parker of the queen's pleasure to have him repair immediately to London. On January 4, Bacon writes that he has been ordered "to haste your coming up" to London. It was not until March 1, 1559, while still urging that he be left alone or at least be put "where ye will else," that his resistance began to weaken. He wrote that he was sorry "to discontent Mr. Secretary and you," and his words of surrender were "do with me what ye will." Later he again pled to be excused, and the interchange of correspondence was brought to an end with two letters signed jointly by Bacon and Cecil.[32]

What Cecil had in mind for Parker was the archbishopric of Canterbury. There were many things to commend the choice, not least of which was the administrative skill Parker had displayed at Stoke-by-Clare, as master of Corpus Christi, and especially during his terms as vice-chancellor of the university.[33] Unfortunately there is not the detailed evidence of Cecil's involvement with regard to other episcopal appointments. Much later Edmund Grindal acknowledged that it was Cecil who was the "principal procurer" of his successive preferments,[34] an acknowledgment given added weight by the care Cecil subsequently took to shield Grindal from the consequences of the queen's displeasure, an endeavor in which Cecil was successful until the very close of Grindal's career.

Further evidence of Cecil's participation in the selection of those to be appointed to episcopal posts is provided by several memoranda among Cecil's papers which indicate that he was busy at an early

32. *Correspondence of Matthew Parker*, pp. 49–53, 57, 68–69. See also Robert Tittler, *Nicholas Bacon: The Making of a Tudor Statesman* (Athens, Ohio, 1976), p. 86.

33. Cecil had exercised equally careful discrimination in recruiting personnel for major posts in the government. Contrary to the expectations of many of his "friends" in exile, neither Anthony Cooke, his father-in-law, nor Thomas Wrothe were given administrative positions. Jewel had written from Strassburg that many believed Cooke would become lord chancellor, but, Jewel added, while "worthy and pious," he is "I think hardly qualified for that office." *Zurich Letters, 1558–1579*, p. 8. For expectations with regard to Wrothe and Cooke, see also ibid., p. 53. Cecil must have concurred in Jewel's opinion of Cooke's administrative talents. As added confirmation of Cecil's judgment one may note that neither Cooke nor Wrothe had been given administrative posts under Edward VI.

34. *Remains of Edmund Grindal, Archbishop of Canterbury* (Cambridge, 1843), p. 402.

date in identifying personnel to serve the church. He did this with some care. The first memorandum lists in one column the names of 26 "spiritual men without preferment at this present" and in another column "benefices and other spiritual promotions presently in the queen's disposition with the value of their livings." The list of "spiritual men" begins with Barlow, Scory, Coverdale (inserted into the list), Cox, Parker, May, Sandys, Cheyney, Whitehead, Sampson, Guest, and Horne. About the only item of interest about the list, which becomes progressively undistinguished, is that practically all those named had been at Cambridge. The memorandum which follows in sequence in the file contains a list of dioceses with the names of Grindal, Cox, Barlow, and Scory in a separate grouping apparently placed opposite the names of London, Norwich, Chichester, and Hereford, sees to which with the exception of Cox they were ultimately appointed. Farther to the right on the sheet is a list of 19 additional names, again almost exclusively of Cambridge men, beginning with Parker, Bill, Whitehead, Pilkington, Sandys, Horne, Sampson, and Jewel. Of the 19 names, 12 are marked with a cross (not an "x"), the cross having been generally interpreted as an indication that these men were singled out to be bishops, since six of those so marked were elevated to the episcopate.[35] The third memorandum, which perhaps antedated the second, is chiefly of interest as further indication of the sorting out and shuffling of possibilities that was taking place, Sampson being shifted from Hereford to Norwich to make room for Scory.[36]

Such activity was appropriate for a principal secretary, especially so for one who took an active interest in religious affairs. It became even more appropriate when members of the council were named "ecclesiastical commissioners." Furthermore, since nominations were processed by Cecil as principal secretary, he was in a position to present counterrecommendations to the queen. It is interesting that long after an episcopate had been provided for the church, complete

35. The last of the 19 names has generally been transcribed Allen but it probably ought to be Alley, an item of little consequence since both belonged to the same Cambridge coterie and both were elected bishops, although Allen died before his consecration.

36. These memoranda are in the Public Record Office where their identifying numbers are State Papers 12/4/38, 12/4/39, and 12/11/12. Strype reproduced the first two memoranda in *Annals of the Reformation* (Oxford, 1824), I, i, 227 f.

with archbishops, individual bishops continued to report to Cecil on the state of their respective dioceses, relating the problems they were encountering, and listing causes both for hope and despair.[37]

37. Instances of such reporting may be found throughout N. H. Birt's accounts of individual dioceses. For John Best's reports which followed a typical pattern, see Birt, *The Elizabethan Religious Settlement* (London, 1907), pp. 310 ff. Even the access of Archbishop Parker to the queen was through Cecil. See, for example, *C.S.P., Domestic, 1547–1580*, p. 142.

VII. THE RELIGIOUS SETTLEMENT OF 1559: PARLIAMENTARY ACTS AND ROYAL INJUNCTIONS

After reviewing the evidence, one can conclude with reasonable assurance that the government managed to secure the adoption of its program for a religious settlement, as represented by the Acts of Supremacy and Uniformity and completed by the Royal Injunctions of 1559, without major modification or alteration. The defect in the "ornaments proviso" of the Act of Uniformity, that was to cause so much trouble in the future, would appear to have been inadvertent rather than calculated and its consequences unanticipated. There is little indication of an obstreperous lobby of militant Protestant extremists in the House of Commons forcing the government to accept a compromise settlement. Evidence points to the upper chamber as the source of the government's problems. Delay and changes in strategy were forced primarily by the intransigence of the lords.[1]

PLANS FOR THE ALTERATION OF RELIGION

Among three surviving letters or memoranda of advice to Elizabeth at the beginning of her reign, the opinion was unanimous that restraint in religious matters must be exercised. Nicholas Throckmorton urged her to move with caution at the outset and to avoid any form of religious innovation. Richard Goodrich, in his "Divers

---

1. Seldom has anyone more completely misread the situation than the Spanish ambassador when he reported on February 20, 1559, that "the queen has entire disposal of the upper chamber in a way never seen before in previous Parliaments, as in this there are several who have hopes of getting her to marry them, and they are careful to please her in all things and persuade others to do the same." *C.S.P., Spanish, 1558–1567*, I, 32. His estimate was a measure of his own anxieties accentuated by uncertainty concerning Elizabeth's intentions. He was undoubtedly correct that had Elizabeth pursued the course he was urging upon her, she could have carried the upper house with her.

points of religion," suggested Elizabeth practice "dissimulation" until Parliament met, and attempt to mislead the papacy by maintaining an agent in Rome and by giving deceptive assurances. Alteration in religion should be deferred until her position was secure, and at her first Parliament the pope's authority should not be touched, nor anything else attempted other than the repeal of the statutes of Henry IV and Henry V so that, freed from usurped ecclesiastical jurisdiction, "quiet persons may live safely" and not be harried by strict enforcement of existing laws. Armagail Waad, in his "Distresses of the commonwealth," also suggested proceeding slowly, especially considering "the greatness of the pope." His advice was to effect change "little by little."[2]

Contrary advice was supplied a few weeks later by an anonymous "Device for alteration of religion," a copy of which was first found in a book of Thomas Smith.[3] The "Device" opens with the recommendation that the "alteration of religion" should be attempted "at the next Parliament," and that a committee should be appointed "to review the book of common prayer." This committee should be composed of "such learned men as be mete to show their minds herein" and competent "to bring a plat or book hereof ready drawn to . . . put into the parliament house." William Bill, Matthew Parker, William May, Richard Cox, David Whitehead, Edmund Grindal, and James Pilkington are suggested as "apt men" for this purpose, and it is proposed that Thomas Smith "do call them together." It is further suggested that certain noblemen—the marquis of Northampton (William Parr), the earl of Bedford (Francis Russell), the earl of Pembroke (William Herbert), and Lord John Grey—"be most fit to be made privy to these proceedings before it be opened to the whole council."[4]

2. The Goodrich and Waad documents are printed in Henry Gee, *The Elizabethan Prayer-Book and Ornaments* (London, 1902), pp. 202–15. For Throckmorton, see "Nicholas Throckmorton's Advice to Queen Elizabeth," *English Historical Review* LXV (1950), 93–98.

3. Gee, *Elizabethan Prayer-Book*, p. 17. The "Device" is printed in ibid., pp. 195–202.

4. Ibid., pp. 200–201. J. E. Neale notes that the "Device" was drafted by December 27, 1558, but to have known that the four exiles—Cox, Whitehead, Grindal, and Pilkington—would soon be in London means that it could not have been drafted much before December 27. Cox was the first to arrive and was probably already in London. Pilkington did not arrive in time to partic-

There is no evidence to indicate that this committee ever met or was even appointed. Still it was a sensible proposal to have an agreed upon plan for the alteration of religion ready to be submitted to Parliament by the Privy Council,5 and it is a proposal that has a certain air of plausibility and ring of authenticity. The members proposed were those used repeatedly in carrying forward religious reforms at the outset of the reign. Such was Smith's relationship to Cecil that the proposal that he convene such a committee and that it meet at his house seems reasonable and appropriate. The suggestion that certain lords "be made privy" to the proceedings prior to any submission to the council is reminiscent of the procedure followed in 1551 at the homes of Richard Morison and William Cecil when some members of the court were briefed in advance so that they would be familiar with the arguments regarding the sacraments. Moreover, the names of the lords who were suggested are as familiar as those of the proposed clerical members. Cecil would probably have made the same choices, and perhaps he did. The "Device" may have been mislaid, forgotten, or ignored. The committee proposed may never have been appointed and, if appointed, may never have met. But what is significant is that the names proposed were the names of those most actively involved in effecting the settlement,

---

ipate in any discussion much before the end of January. See Neale, "The Elizabethan Acts of Supremacy and Uniformity," *English Historical Review* LXV (1950): 305.

5. Neale makes two curious comments about the "Device." First, he suggests that such a committee was unnecessary for on December 23 a committee had already been appointed by the privy council "for the consideration of what things necessary in Parliament." Neale forgets momentarily that this was a committee of technicians composed of the lord great seal, the judges, the sergeants-at-law, the attorney general, the solicitor general, and Thomas Smith and Richard Goodrich, a civilian and a common lawyer. Their commission was to make the necessary arrangements for Parliament, not to draft a program for Parliament. The second curious comment is that since Smith and Goodrich, as lawyers, were "capable of dealing with ecclesiastical matters" and were members of the Privy Council committee, "I do not think we need to invent any second committee" to deal with the alteration of religion" (*English Historical Review* LXV [1950]: 306). This statement is made doubly curious when, two pages later, Neale comments: "With the Marian bishops . . . entrenched in the upper house, where the lay peers could not match them in theological debate, . . . the main assault on the Catholic church was bound to be opened in the commons." Ibid., p. 308.

and more important the policy proposed, in contrast to the suggestion in the other memoranda of delaying action and proceeding slowly step-by-step, was the policy adopted.

The author of the "Device" urged a full and complete alteration of religion as soon as Parliament met. He was aware of the dangers. "The bishop of Rome will be incensed." "The French king will be encouraged more to war." "Many people of our own will be much discontented." Disaffection would arise from various quarters, but the most serious would come from many who "would gladly have the alteration from the church of Rome" but who, when they discovered that "some old ceremonies shall be left still, or that their doctrine which they embrace is not allowed and . . . all other abolished . . . , shall be discontented and call the alteration a *cloaked papistry* or a *mingle-mangle*." This was the greater danger, for it would threaten the unity and tranquility of the realm. The only way to deal with this danger was to proceed with dispatch at the forthcoming Parliament, the sooner the better. "For the discontentation of such as could be content to have religion altered but would have it go too far, the strait laws upon the promulgation of the [prayer] book and severe execution of the same at the first will so repress them that it is a great hope it shall touch but a few. And better it were that they did suffer than her highness or commonwealth should shake or be in danger."[6] Whoever the author may have been, he remembered the contentions under Edward VI as well as "the troubles at Frankfort." He also was prophetic. By May 22, as a result of the delay in the taking of "other order" as envisaged in the "proviso" of the Act of Uniformity, Jewel had begun to call attention to the consequence. "We have at this time, not only to contend with our adversaries, but even with those of our friends who, of later years, have fallen away from us and gone over to the opposite party, and

6. Gee, *Elizabethan Prayer-Book*, pp. 197, 200. The stress on avoiding undue delay in establishing a firm settlement is reminiscent of Thomas Cranmer's letter of October 7, 1552, urging the council in similar fashion to act with firmness. "I know your lordships' wisdom to be such that I trust ye will not be moved by the glorious and unquiet spirits which can like nothing but that [which] is after their own fancy and cease not to make trouble and disquietness when things be most quiet and in good order. If such men should be heard, although the book were made every year, yet should it not lack faults in their opinion." Ibid., pp. 225–26.

who are now opposing us with a bitterness and obstinacy far exceeding that of any common enemy."[7]

When Parliament met on January 25, 1559, it immediately became clear that the type of thinking represented by the "Device" had become official government policy. When the queen arrived at Westminster Abbey, where the two houses had assembled for the opening sermon, it was Richard Cox who ascended the pulpit and began his sermon with praise for Elizabeth, whose mission was to purify the church. According to Il Schifanoya, the free-lance agent of the Mantuan ambassador resident in Brussels, Cox told the queen that "God had given her this dignity to the end that she might no longer allow or tolerate the past iniquities" which he had enumerated, exhorted her "to destroy the images of the saints," and said "many other things against the Christian religion." The sermon, which also reminded the Parliament of its duty, lasted for an hour and a half, with "the peers standing the whole time."[8]

Following the sermon, the assemblage moved to the lord's chamber in the parliament house where, in the presence of the queen, Nicholas Bacon spoke for the government and outlined the agenda for Elizabeth's first Parliament. Bacon stressed as the first of three priorities the need for "the well-making of laws" to unite "these people of the realm into an uniform order of religion" and to avoid whatever might tend to breed or nurture idolatry and superstition. Bacon concluded with an eloquent appeal. "Forced by our duties to God, . . . drawn by our love to our country, encouraged by so princely a patroness, let us in God's name go about this work, endeavoring ourselves with all diligence . . . to make such laws as may tend to the honor and glory of God, to the establishment of his church, and to the tranquility of the realm."[9]

7. *Zurich Letters, 1558–1579*, p. 32. Jewel probably had in mind, among others, the Levers of St. John's who had defected to the Genevan camp. He also may have had Sampson in mind, for the latter had become increasingly restive.

8. *C.S.P., Venetian, 1558–1570*, VII, 23.

9. Simonds D'Ewes, *The Journals of All the Parliaments during the Reign of Queen Elizabeth* (Shannon, 1973), pp. 11–12. Count de Feria, using "they" to set forth Bacon's three points, took it for granted that Bacon's address represented the government's agenda. *C.S.P., Spanish, 1558–1567*, I, 25.

This was the mandate, but translating the rhetoric into legislation was conditioned by at least two very practical considerations.

The first circumstance to be taken into account was the importance of making peace with France, if for no other reason than to make the Scottish border secure and to minimize any potential threat to Elizabeth's position represented by a rival claim of Mary Stuart to the throne. John Mason's memorandum of November 20, 1558, had emphasized that "peace is the first and principal object" to be pursued, and his counsel had been echoed in other memoranda of advice at the beginning of Elizabeth's reign. Later the Spanish ambassador noted that "these heretics that surround" Elizabeth seek to persuade her that "she has sufficient strength of her own to defend herself against the French," but he had warned her of the "inability" of the English "to stand alone against the French" and that, if the attempt were made, "the French would eat them up."[10]

The necessity of retaining a modicum of Spanish support until peace with France had been secured must have been the reason for much of the dissimulation practiced by Elizabeth. No matter what Parliament did, she still possessed the power of veto. She was in a position, therefore, to endeavor to calm Spanish apprehensions and encourage Spanish hopes and thus facilitate the making of peace with France by not alienating the Spanish prematurely. It is in this light that one can understand Elizabeth's elation on March 19 when she was able to tell Count de Feria bluntly, for the first time, that she could not and would not marry the Spanish king. With peace with France concluded, she also was ready to lend her support to vigorous action to reach a religious settlement. Edmund Grindal put it succinctly when he wrote to a friend two months later: "We were indeed urgent from the very first that a general reformation should take place. But the Parliament long delayed the matter . . . until a peace had been concluded between . . . the French king and ourselves."[11]

The second circumstance which served to determine the timing and strategy to be pursued in effecting a religious settlement was the necessity of securing the approval of both Houses of Parliament. The Commons posed no problem. The complicating factor was the

10. *C.S.P., Domestic, 1547–1560* (London, 1856), p. 115; *C.S.P, Spanish, 1558–1567*, I, 34–35.
11. *Zurich Letters, 1558–1602*, Second series, p. 19.

intransigence of the Lords created in part, as John Jewel reported in a letter to Peter Martyr in Zurich, by the presence of the Marian bishops in the upper chamber. "The bishops are a great hindrance to us, for being, as you know, among the nobility and leading men in the upper house, and having none there on our side to expose their artifices and confute their falsehoods, they reign as sole monarchs" among "ignorant and weak men, and easily overreach our little party, either by their numbers or their reputation for learning." [12]

In the beginning the government was restrained from making any frontal attack upon the bishops both by the dictates of the peace negotiations and by the not unreasonable hope that some of them, having previously adjusted to Henry VIII's break with Rome and to the Edwardian reforms, could be persuaded to accept another reversal of religious policy. Securing the acquiescence of only two or three men of stature, such as Cuthbert Tunstall and Nicholas Heath, who were as accustomed to the service of the government as they were of the church, would weaken the conservative faction, solidify the position of the new regime, and ease the problem of consecrating new bishops. The hope, however reasonable, proved illusory, and in the end only Anthony Kitchin of Llandaff conformed, an obscure and less than notable catch. [13]

In contrast to the intransigence encountered by the government in the upper chamber, the House of Commons was capable of functioning smoothly, efficiently, and speedily. Quick action was possible because of a unified leadership that was strong in numbers, experience, and ability. Two-thirds of the House were members for the first time, and care had been exercised in their selection. Francis Russell, earl of Bedford, for example, was active in the west-

---

12. *Zurich Letters, 1558–1579*, p. 10. Convocation was in session, meeting simultaneously with Parliament, and as representative of the old regime it was bending every effort to stiffen the resistance to change of the upper chamber. For the activities of convocation at this time, see W. P. Haugaard, *Elizabeth and the English Reformation* (Cambridge, 1968), pp. 62, 87–88, 238.

13. The bishop of Aquila reported to Philip of Spain on July 12, 1559: "I understand that the bishop of Llandaff, who is a greedy old man with but little learning, is wavering, and it is feared he may take the oath as he is wearing a bishop's garb again lately. I had news of this and sent to visit him and console him as well as I could, but he has given way notwithstanding. The rest of them are firm . . . , and they hope more than ever in your Majesty." *C.S.P., Spanish, 1558–1567*, I, 866.

ern counties in securing seats for godly Protestants, and Ambrose Cave became chancellor of the duchy of Lancaster on December 28, 1558, in ample time to influence the representation for Lancashire. Seats were secured for Cecil's clerk-secretary Roger Alford, for his estate manager John Purvey (Magdalen Cheke's husband), and for his old friends Thomas Smith and John Thynne, as well as for his neighbor and friend Walter Mildmay.[14] Seats also were found for a dozen exiles, including Francis Knollys and Cecil's late-returning father-in-law, Anthony Cooke. The experienced one-third of the membership was heavily laced with government representatives, perhaps fifty in all. All the commoners in the Privy Council had seats, as did other persons holding government and household posts of some consequence. They were the official nucleus and were able to exert great influence.[15]

On February 9, two weeks after the opening of Parliament, the government bill "to restore the supremacy of the church of England, etc., to the crown of the realm" was introduced in the Commons. Little is known of the legislative history of the bill. No text of it, as introduced or as brought back from committee on February 21, has survived. The journal of the House is tantalizingly uninformative. Anthony Cooke was impatient. Three days after the bill was introduced Cooke complained to Peter Martyr that "we are moving far too slowly," but he acknowledged that "the result of this meeting of Parliament will, as far as I can judge, confirm my hope."[16] The following day, February 13, the bill received a second reading. It was debated the next day, and then on February 15 the bill was referred to Francis Knollys and Anthony Cooke, supposedly for revision. When Knollys and Cooke reported back on February 21, the bill, which presumably had been designed as a simple Act of Supremacy, had been expanded, by the inclusion of a revised prayer

14. See Wallace MacCaffrey, *The Shaping of the Elizabethan Regime* (Princeton, 1968), pp. 53–55; and especially John C. Roberts, "Parliamentary Representation in Devon and Dorset, 1159–1601," unpublished University of London M.A. thesis cited by MacCaffrey. For Alford and Purvey, see R. C. Barnett, *Place, Profit, and Power: A Study of the Servants of William Cecil* (Chapel Hill, 1969), pp. 26, 111.

15. Even before it was known how extensive the canvassing had been, Conyers Read noted that men of long experience and ability, supported by a popular queen, could do much to direct a house, two-thirds of which had never sat before. Read, *Mr. Secretary Cecil*, p. 130.

16. *Zurich Letters, 1558–1602*, Second series, 13–14.

book, to become a bill embodying an Act of Supremacy and Uni-formity. The House then acted with dispatch. The new or expanded bill was given a first reading on February 21 with "little or no debate." It was read a second time the next day. Cecil rarely showed his hand, but on February 25, according to the Spanish ambassador, Cecil cracked the whip by getting up a "wrangle" to stop further discussion and to carry out his "wicked plan." Since the bill was sent for engrossing without a further committee, it is evident that whatever opposition there may have been was effectively quelled and the bill as brought in by Knollys and Cooke was adopted with-out amendment.[17]

What can we learn from this simple account? The major lesson is that the government could marshal an effective majority for deci-sive action when it was ready to do so. The question remains, how-ever, why was there a change in strategy on February 15? We know that Cooke thought things were moving too slowly and it is possible that others among those whom Jewel referred to as "our friends" were restive.[18] Cooke apparently shared the conviction of the author of the "Device" that a quick settlement was necessary to put a stop

17. *C.S.P., Spanish, 1558–67*, I, 33, 37. Neale, *English Historical Review* LXV (1950): 314, 319. The sequence of events from February 9 to February 25 illustrate the limitations imposed upon any attempt to flesh out the story in detail. There is no surviving text of the original bill introduced on February 9 which was sent to committee on February 15. Nor is there a text of the bill reported back from the committee on February 21, although it is known from the debate it kindled that it had been expanded to include a basis for uniformity of worship as well as the restoration of the royal supremacy. Two other items were mentioned in the Commons journal on February 15 and 16—"The Bill for the Order of Service and Ministers in the Church," and "The Book of Common Prayer and Ministration of the Sacraments." No text of these survives to explain what may have been afoot. It is possible that they may have been referred to the same committee for consideration, since nothing more is heard of them. In this situation, it is folly to posit some *specific clause* of any of these bills as a basis for explaining what was intended on a specific date.

18. The term "our friends" represented no clearly defined group. Jewel uses it casually in his letters to Peter Martyr. Usually he mentions Grindal, Sandys, Cox, Parker, Horne, Sampson, Scory, and Barlow within this cate-gory, but the frequency is mainly determined by what he has to report. He also includes Allen, Aylmer, and Guest as being identified with the others. And he considers Cecil, Cooke, and Wrothe as being friends. If it were pos-sible to ask him what he meant by "our friends," he probably might add others—for example, Knollys and Bacon. See *Zurich Letters, 1558–1579*, 6, 10, 11, 13, 15, 18, 20, 23, 27, 40, 48, 51, 53, 55, 58, 59, 63, 69, 72, 79, 93.

to such dissension as developed under Edward and at Frankfort. Cecil, on the other hand, could count votes and knew that the bill would not have a chance of being passed by the upper chamber.

There are two possible explanations for the change in strategy. First, it may have been concluded that it was necessary to deal with restiveness among the government's supporters by demonstrating that it was not yet possible to secure favorable action in the House of Lords. Second, it may have been concluded that the bill would serve the useful function of forcing individual members of the upper chamber to disclose their position and thus make it easier to identify points of weakness in opposition ranks as well as those who were most intransigent. The government would thus be better able to determine what countermeasures needed to be taken to gain a majority vote in the upper house. Whatever the reason for forcing the issue, the House of Lords, as was predictable, dismantled the measure.

The expanded Commons bill for supremacy and uniformity[19] was taken to the Lords on February 27, given a first reading on February 28, and was then laid aside until March 13 when it was read a second time and committed to a committee for revision. With Parliament scheduled to end on March 24 before Easter, this would appear to have been a deliberate tactic of delay. The bill was returned on March 15 sheared of everything except provision for the royal supremacy, and was read for the first time. It was given a second reading on March 17 and committed for engrossing, being read for a third time and passed on March 18. Even as revised, all the bishops and two of the temporal lords voted against the bill.

Il Schifanoya reported to the Mantuan ambassador that "the members of the lower house," when it became apparent what the Lords were doing, "grew angry" because "they must of necessity ratify what they had done in the upper house." Time had run out. Members of the Commons had either to forego abolishing papal jurisdiction or accept the Lords' purged version of the Commons' bill. Neale notes that the members of the Commons were "defiant" and that

19. Neale suggests that the expanded bill revived several Edwardian acts, including the 1552 Act of Uniformity and others relating to the use of images, the sacrament of the altar, and the marriage of priests, by the simple device of repealing Mary's 1553 statute which had repealed them. *English Historical Review* LXV (1950): 316–17.

they "expressed their defiance" on March 17 by introducing a bill "that no person shall be punished for using the religion used in king E.'s last year," a bill which was read twice that morning, read a third time the next day and adopted. It was brought to the Lords on Monday, March 20, and that was the end of it.[20]

The purged supremacy bill was brought back to the Commons on March 18, was adopted with a proviso, returned to the Lords where it in turn was altered, and then was approved by both houses on March 22 and was ready for the royal assent. A proclamation was issued, dated March 22, which noted that Easter was at hand and that great numbers wished to receive communion in both kinds as authorized by the supremacy bill passed by both houses of Parliament.[21] Since the act was too long to be printed in time, the proclamation stated that "the statute of Edward VI for communion in both kinds, revived in the supremacy act, is declared to be revived and in full force.[22]

By this time, the government was beginning to play out a charade. The act had not yet been signed. Elizabeth was to appear on March 24 to give her assent and to declare Parliament dissolved. Instead she withheld her assent and declared the Parliament to be recessed until April 3, after Easter.[23]

20. *C.S.P., Venetian, 1558–1570*, VII, 52–53.

21. The purged bill, as finally adopted, had acquired a dangling provision for communion in both kinds. J. E. Neale, for some reason, believed that this dangling provision was a survival from the original bill of February 9 and that it provided the "vital clue" for understanding what was originally intended. It would seem much more reasonable to assume that this dangling provision for communion in both kinds was the "proviso" of March 18 and that it was directly related to Elizabeth's proclamation of March 22 authorizing the reception of communion in both kinds on Easter Sunday. For a critique of Neale's interpretation of the clause, see C. W. Dugmore, *The Mass and the English Reformers* (London, 1958), pp. 210–11.

22. Neale, *English Historical Review* LXV (1950): 323.

23. The confusion is illustrated by a report on March 24 of Count de Feria: "Last night the queen sent to say she would see me at 9 o'clock this morning, and just as I was ready to go a message came for me to put off my visit as she was very busy. She had resolved to go to Parliament today at 1 o'clock after dinner *and there, all being assembled, to confirm what they had agreed to in the matters they have discussed, although I do not know for certain what this is.* Her going was, however postponed till next Monday week, the third of April." *C.S.P., Spanish, 1558–1567*, I, 44 (italics added). Neale cites this passage as evidence that Elizabeth changed her mind about signing the supremacy bill on the night of March 23, *English Historical*

What brought about the decision announced on Good Friday, March 24, 1559, to continue the Parliament instead of bringing it to an end as previously planned? Three weeks later John Jewel explained a basic concern of the government's policy.

> This woman [Elizabeth], excellent as she is and earnest in the cause of religion, nothwithstanding she desires a thorough change as early as possible, cannot however be induced to effect such a change without the sanction of the law lest the matter should seem to have been accomplished, not so much by the judgment of discrete men, as in compliance with the impulse of a furious multitude.[24]

Jewel further explained that the earlier inaction had stemmed "only from the circumstances of the times." The first of these circumstances was the lack of peace with France. The second was the hope that some of the more moderate Marian bishops could be induced to acquiesce in the alteration of religion. By March 24 peace with France had been achieved, and the bishops, exercising a veto power in the House of Lords, had played out their hand. While the hope of being able to retain at least two or three of the bishops was not entirely abandoned, the decision to continue Parliament represented a drastic change in policy.

The change in tactics was no spur-of-the-moment decision. While the two houses, faced with a March 24 dissolution, were engaged in a struggle to gain whatever little advantage could be gained by last-ditch adjustments, a new strategy was being devised and implemented. Elizabeth knew of the French treaty by March 19 when she

---

Review LXV (1950): 324. Actually, all the statement says is that she was going to Parliament to confirm publicly what "they" had discussed and upon which "they" were agreed, evidently a change of some sort that may have been agreed upon two, three, or four days earlier. But she did not go to Parliament and "with all being assembled" make a public announcement of "the matters" of which the Spanish ambassador was ignorant. She was apparently "very busy" the morning of March 24 because questions were being raised about the wisdom of publicly disclosing the decision that had been reached one, two, three, or even four days earlier. The proclamation, dated March 22, had been printed in advance, and therefore does not preclude a decision to withhold the queen's assent and to pursue a new strategy having been reached a day or two earlier.

24. *Zurich Letters, 1558–1579*, p. 18.

could not conceal her elation from Count de Feria as she excitedly told him that she was a heretic. By March 20 Jewel knew of plans for a conference at Westminster, knew the names of those selected to be participants, and knew that the disputation was to be used to reduce the effectiveness of the opposition of the Marian bishops to liturgical reform by removing the debate to a forum where their arguments could be successfully countered. Another indicator that a shift had been in process of being planned was the appointment of William Bill, Richard Cox, and Robert Horne to preach the traditional St. Mary's 'Spital sermons, with Thomas Sampson giving the "rehearsal sermon" (summaries of the three other sermons ending with an exhortation of his own) at Paul's Cross.[25] These sermons represented the first authorized preaching, except for Parker's sermon of February 10 at Paul's Cross, outside the royal chapel since December. They were to precede the beginning of the disputation in Westminster Abbey and they obviously signaled the opening salvo of a concerted propaganda campaign.

The Westminster disputation scheduled for the Easter recess was staged as a public show to win support for the program of religious change by putting the Marian bishops on the defensive, discrediting their arguments, and thus eroding their support and possibly silencing them.[26] Members of the council and the Houses of Parliament, as well as "a great number of people of all sorts," were present in the Abbey for the debate. The focus was on three immediately pertinent issues: the use of a language in worship unknown to the worshippers, the power of national churches to determine their own liturgy, and the question of any propitiatory sacrifice in the mass. Nicholas Bacon and Nicholas Heath were

25. These sermons were given at the pulpit cross outside St. Mary's hospital, Bishopsgate, on Monday, Tuesday, and Wednesday following Easter. The rehearsal sermon of the following Sunday, "Low Sunday," was customarily given at Paul's Cross. See Millar Maclure, *The Paul's Cross Sermons* (Toronto, 1958), p. 9.

26. There were to be either eight or nine participants on each side. Those representing what Jewel called "our side" were John Aylmer, Richard Cox, Edmund Grindal, Edmund Guest, Robert Horne, John Jewel, John Scory, David Whitehead, and possibly Edwin Sandys. Roman Catholics appointed by Nicholas Heath to participate were the bishops of Chester (Cuthbert Scot), Coventry and Lichfield (Ralph Bayne), Lincoln (Thomas Watson), Winchester (John White), and possibly Carlisle (Owen Oglethorpe), and four "doctors"—Cole, dean of St. Paul's; Chedsey, archdean of Middlesex; Harpsfield, archdeacon of Canterbury; and Langdale, archdeacon of Lewes.

joint chairmen, but Bacon acted as the moderator who enforced the prearranged rules that Roman Catholic participants should speak first and participants should present written statements.

The conference became somewhat of a shambles, for the Roman Catholic participants perhaps did not fully understand the agreed procedures. The dean of St. Paul's led off on the first day without a prepared paper, while Horne responded with a written and carefully argued defense of a vernacular liturgy. The second day never got beyond procedural wrangling, with the Roman Catholic participants in frustration resorting to verbal abuse and refusing to speak first rather than last. The bishops of Lincoln and Winchester were sent to the Tower for contempt, and their colleagues were heavily fined, and ordered to remain in the city and report daily to the council. The confinement of Watson and White reduced the bishops' attendance in the House of Lords by at least two, and the public intimidation may have accounted for two additional absentees. More important, according to Jewel, the extreme behavior of the Marian churchmen had cost them the sympathy of many, especially among the nobility.[27] There was a sufficient shift of opinion to allow the supremacy and uniformity bills to pass the Commons without dissent, and the more controversial uniformity bill to squeeze through the Lords on April 29 by the very narrow margin of 3 votes with the 9 bishops present voting solidly against it.[28] On

27. *Zurich Letters, 1558–1579*, p. 18. For descriptions of the "antics" at the disputation, see ibid., pp. 13–16, 27–28.

28. A new supremacy bill, giving Elizabeth the title of "supreme governor," was introduced in the Commons on April 10. The more controversial uniformity bill, proposing the adoption of the 1552 prayer book, was put forward in the Commons on April 18, given a second and third reading and passed on April 19. The passage of both bills through the Lords was completed on April 29.

Seven bishops and John Feckenham, the abbot of Westminster, were not present when the Lords voted on the uniformity bill. Feckenham was strangely absent, having been present the preceding day and was present on the first day of May. Two of the bishops—Watson and White—were in the Tower as an aftermath of the disputation. Bourne of Bath and Wells had been present earlier but had returned to his diocese. Morgan of St. David's and Poole of Peterborough were ill. Goldwell of St. Asaph, had been named to Oxford, and had not been summoned to the parliament, presumably on the basis of his being "in process of translation." Tunstall of Durham was not summoned, being excused by the queen because of his extreme age.

Even after the vote of April 29, Cecil still sought to persuade some of the bishops to conform. Heath of York, Tunstall of Durham, Thirlby of Ely,

May 8, 1559, Elizabeth gave her assent to both bills and Parliament was dissolved.

There was one item of unfinished business of the religious settlement. The speedy approval of the uniformity bill by the House of Lords was purchased at a price, the price being the addition of the so-called ornaments proviso. As part of the official legislative enactment, it was prefixed to the prayer books which were being hastily printed to be ready for use throughout the land on Midsummer Day, June 24, 1559, the Feast of St. John the Baptist. The proviso read as follows:

> Provided always and be it enacted, that such ornaments of the church and of the ministers thereof shall be retained and be in use as was in this Church of England . . . in the second year of the reign of King Edward VI, *until other order shall be therein taken by the authority of the Queen's Majesty with the advice of her commissioners appointed . . . for causes ecclesiastical or of the metropolitan of this realm.*[29]

In order to avoid delay in the House of Lords and to secure the passage of the uniformity bill by that shaky margin of three votes, the question of what Jewel called "the scenic apparatus of divine worship" was left for future determination.[30]

Jewel, writing to Peter Martyr, reveals his own dismay at this

---

Bourne of Bath and Wells, and Kitchin of Llandaff were among those for whom he had greatest hope. In the end Kitchin alone belatedly conformed.

29. Italics added. The Privy Council inserted (this is a reasonable assumption although the Privy Council records are missing for this period) the "proviso" as a rubric in the prayer book when it was printed, omitting the "until" clause but adding "according to the Act of Parliament set in the beginning of this book," *thus indicating by reference to the act the conditional status of the rubric.*

30. Nothing up to this point indicates that Elizabeth was concerned with the issue of ornaments. Bypassing the issue in the bill of uniformity was in deference to divisions within the House of Lords. It is likely that there were at least some who agreed with Armagail Waad that it would be best to proceed "little by little" to avoid as much as possible disturbance created by outward changes. This feeling of caution was in contrast to the belief that it would be far better to make the alteration clearcut at the outset and thus nip in the bud the development of dissension. By setting the issue of ornaments to one side, one can imagine that it was possible to avoid prolonged debate and to secure the two or more votes necessary to pass the bill without delay.

turn of events which left the whole matter of ornaments open and subject to agitation.

> As to religion, it has been effected, I hope under good auspices, that it shall be restored to the same state as it was during your latest residence among us under Edward. But, as far as I can see at present, there is not the same alacrity among our friends as there lately was among the papists. So miserably is it ordered that falsehood is armed. . . . The scenic apparatus of divine worship is now under agitation: and those very things which you and I have so often laughed at are now seriously and solemnly entertained by certain persons (for *we* are not consulted) as if the Christian religion could not exist without something tawdry. Our minds indeed are not sufficiently disengaged to make these fooleries of much importance. Others are seeking after a *golden*, or as it rather seems to me, a *leaden* mediocrity; and are crying out that the half is better than the whole.[31]

Edwin Sandys may or may not have been consulted, but at least he had been reassured. He wrote to Matthew Parker on April 30, 1559, the day after the final passage of the bill through the House of Lords:

> The last book of service is gone through with a proviso to retain the ornaments which were used in the first and second year of King Edward until it please the queen to take other order for them. Our gloss upon this text is that we shall not be forced to use them but that others in the meantime shall not convey them away, but that they may remain for the queen [to take action].[32]

A PROVISO, ROYAL INJUNCTIONS, AND VISITATIONS

Those with qualms about the proviso did not have long to wait. Everything was done in due order, but it was done with some dispatch. There was to be no metropolitan until almost the end of the year when Matthew Parker was consecrated archbishop of Canterbury. Still Elizabeth was not deterred thereby from proceeding to

31. *Zurich Letters, 1558–1579*, p. 23.
32. *Correspondence of Matthew Parker*, p. 65.

reorder and reconstitute the church. She made use of the powers vested in her as "supreme governor" of the church by the Act of Supremacy. On May 23, 1559, just fifteen days after the Act of Supremacy received the queen's assent, a commission was issued under the great seal constituting the members of the Privy Council (Wotton was not included) "ecclesiastical commissioners" to administer the oath of supremacy to all officeholders specified in the act—the bishops, the clergy, the judges, and the justices of the peace. The commissioners gave their initial attention to the surviving Marian bishops, all of whom refused to take the oath, and all of whom, save Kitchin, were deprived between May 29 and the first week of November.33

On June 13, 1559, Cecil wrote to Nicholas Throckmorton in Paris that "the queen is determined, by the advice of her council, to have a great visitation [of the churches] throughout the realm: whereupon the injunctions and articles of inquisition are already formed."34 On June 25, 1559, letters patent were issued to a commission of fourteen to carry out the visitation of the North to impose the prayer book on the churches and to bring both clergy and parishes into conformity with the Royal Injunctions, the situation being ascertained through responses to the Articles of Inquiry. Subsequently commissions were appointed for other sections of the country. On July 19, 1559, a continuing "ecclesiastical commission" for the whole country, which served in part as a court of appeals, was established by the queen "for carrying into execution the acts for the uniformity of common prayer and for restoring to the crown the ancient jurisdiction of the state ecclesiastical."35

The Royal Injunctions were wide-ranging and covered almost all aspects of parish life in 53 numbered directives and 4 additional

33. Kitchin signed a "curious paper" on July 18 which was accepted in lieu of the oath. See R. W. Dixon, *History of the Church of England* (Oxford, 1902), V, 122.

34. *C.S.P., Foreign, 1558–1559*, p. 313. As soon as the Royal Injunctions and Articles of Inquiry were printed, Cecil promised to send "copies thereof" to Throckmorton.

35. *C.S.P., Domestic, 1547–1580*, pp. 132, 134. The letters patent directing the northern visitation and the writ establishing the permanent ecclesiastical commission are printed in Henry Gee, *The Elizabethan Clergy and the Settlement of Religion, 1558–1564* (Oxford, 1898), pp. 89–93, 147–52. Gee also gives the full text of the Royal Injunctions and Articles of Inquiry. Ibid., pp. 46–70.

Injunctions set apart at the end of the document, perhaps for special emphasis. The Injunctions were part of the fundamental law of the religious settlement as authorized by the Act of Supremacy, and were so recognized both at the time and on later occasions.[36] They were issued by the queen, with "the advice of her most honorable council," were presented to all her "loving subjects" as her will and command, "straitly charging and commanding them to observe and keep the same." Penalties, including the queen's "displeasure," are provided and enumerated. Bishops or others "having ecclesiastical jurisdiction, whom her majesty has appointed or shall appoint for the due execution of the same," are charged and commanded to see these Injunctions observed and kept of all persons being under their jurisdiction, as they will answer to her majesty for the contrary." It is further "her highness's pleasure" that "every justice of peace, being required, shall assist" in "the due execution of the said Injunctions." To the extent that the Injunctions dealt with "ornaments," its directives represented the taking of "other order" envisaged in the "ornaments proviso" and served to confirm the reassurance Sandys had received at the time the bill for uniformity cleared both houses of Parliament.

The Injunctions specifically condemned all "works devised by man's fantasies" as "wandering of pilgrimages, setting up of candles, praying upon beads, or such like superstition," since they are "things tending to idolatry and superstition, which of all other offenses God Almighty doth most detest and abhor." The clergy shall do nothing "to set forth or extol the dignity of any images, relics, or miracles" and shall declare their abuse by teaching that "all goodness, health, and grace" should be "looked for only of God." Moreover, those in authority in each parish "shall take away, utterly extinct, and destroy all shrines, coverings of shrines, all tables, candlesticks, trindals, and rolls of wax, pictures, paintings, and all other monuments of feigned miracles, pilgrimages, idolatry, and superstition, so that there remain no memory of the same in walls, glass windows, or elsewhere within their churches and houses."[37] In addition, no

36. See Gee, *The Elizabethan Clergy*, p. 45.
37. The second article of inquiry to be asked in the visitation was "whether in their churches and chapels all images, shrines, all tables, candlesticks, trindals, or rolls of wax, pictures, paintings, and all other monuments of feigned and false miracles, pilgrimages, idolatry, and superstition be removed, abolished, and destroyed."

private persons shall "keep in their houses any abused images, tables, pictures, paintings, and other monuments of feigned miracles, pilgrimages, idolatry, and superstition."

The Injunctions note that the altars have been removed and replaced with tables in many churches, while in other churches the altars have not yet been removed awaiting "some order therein to be taken by her majesty's visitors." With regard to this, "saving for an uniformity, there seems no matter of great moment, so that the Sacrament be duly and reverently ministered." On the other hand, "for observation of one uniformity through the whole realm, and for the better imitation of the law in that behalf, it is ordered that no altar be taken down but by oversight of the curate of the church and the churchwardens, or one of them at the least, wherein no riotous or disordered manner [is] to be used." It is also ordered that "the holy table in every church be decently made and set in the place where the altar stood," except when communion is to be administered, at which time it shall be placed within the chancel where "the minister may be more conveniently heard of the communicants" and "the communicants also more conveniently and in more number communicate. Afterward the table shall be placed where it stood before."38

The portion of the Injunctions dealing with clerical dress was subject to misinterpretation by some of the churchwardens. For the sake of being held in outward reverence, all "admitted into any vocation ecclesiastical, or into any society of learning in either of the universities or elsewhere, shall use and wear such seemly habits, garments, and square caps, as were most commonly and orderly received in the latter year of King Edward VI." This is ambiguous. It could be interpreted as the conventional daily garb in contrast to vestments used in public worship. The latter were mentioned in a subsequent directive which ordered "the churchwardens of every parish" to "deliver unto our visitors the inventories of vestments, copes, and other ornaments, plate, books, and specially of grails, couchers, legends, processionals, manuals, hymnals, portasses, and such like appertaining to their church."

The Injunctions also dealt with the issue posed by Elizabeth's

38. Although stated ambiguously, the intent is clear that, for uniformity's sake, altars should be removed. The injunction concerning sacramental bread also is confused, but it is clear that it is to be bread and not a wafer. The phrase "as the usual bread and water" adds to the confusion.

supposed attitude toward married clergy.[39] Sandys had written Parker on April 30, 1559, noting that Lever had married and then commented: "The queen's majesty will wink at it but not establish it by law, which is nothing else but to bastard our children."[40] Sandys was wrong, for as part of the general religious settlement represented by the Injunctions, clerical marriage was both established and regulated.

Following the issuance of letters patent and a period of preparation, the visitations began early in August. Jewel wrote on August 1, 1559, that he was setting out upon a long and troublesome commission as the clerical member of the commission for the southwest, and on November 2 he reported that he had just returned. Sandys was away for the same length of time with the visitation of the north. Sandys reported that all images had been taken down, and similar testimony was given by Jewel and Cox. Much earlier, on August 13, the Spanish ambassador wrote that "they have just taken away the crosses, images, and altars from St. Paul's and all the other London churches." Since these visitors also had responsibility for East Anglia, they apparently handled London with dispatch before moving to the eastern counties. The visitations were generally concluded in October when a writ was issued for the formal suspension of the powers of the visitors, with permission being granted to conclude some causes still in progress.

The subscription devised for the visitation was designed to make an adjustment to the alteration of religion as easy as possible for tender consciences. What was required, Henry Gee noted, was not "the supremacy oath pure and simple, but *a summary form of subscription to the settlement of religion as set out in the Supremacy Act, the Uniformity Act, and the Injunctions.*" The clergy were

39. Elizabeth seldom seemed happy when anyone got married, but the rude remark to Parker's wife attributed to her sounds apocryphal. If she was opposed to clerical marriage at this early date, her conviction was not very strong. With only two or three exceptions, all her early bishops, deans, chaplains, and even her almoner were married. A hardened hostility to clerical marriage came later after she had become alienated by the forwardness of the bishops in taking a collective stance on several matters, and Elizabeth seems to have used the marriage issue to embarrass them and indicate her displeasure. See *Correspondence of Matthew Parker*, pp. 148, 156–57.

40. Ibid., p. 66. The words "wink at" are reminiscent of Richard Goodrich's legal advice submitted at the outset of Elizabeth's reign. See Gee, *The Elizabethan Prayer-book*, p. 205.

asked to "confess and acknowledge" that "the ancient jurisdiction over the state ecclesiastical" had been restored to the crown, and "all foreign power repugnant to the same" had been abolished "according to an oath thereof made in the late Parliament." The clergy were asked to "confess also and acknowledge" that the prayer book and "the orders and rules contained in the Injunctions" were "according to the true word of God and agreeable to the doctrine of the primitive church."[41]

41. Gee, *The Elizabethan Clergy*, pp. 45, 78.

VIII. THE RELIGIOUS SETTLEMENT OF 1559: ELIZABETH AND THE ROYAL PREROGATIVE

A final conclusion one may reach with reasonable assurance is two-fold. First, Elizabeth was the consistent friend of those who upheld the 1552 prayer book during the months it was under consideration. Second, her disaffection with them at the point of "ornaments" came later and was based upon what she considered to be a defense of her royal prerogative.

ELIZABETH'S RELIGIOUS VIEWS

Elizabeth acquiesced in the selection of William Bill to preach at Paul's Cross on the Sunday following her accession, in the selection of Richard Cox to preach at the opening of Parliament, in the choice of zealous Protestants (all of whom, except Parker, were exiles under Mary) to preach in the royal chapel during Lent and to preach the 'Spital sermons during the week after Easter as well as in the naming of those who were to present the government's position in the Westminster disputation, in the selection of Edmund Grindal to interpret the prayer book at Paul's Cross when it was imposed by the Act of Uniformity, and in drawing upon these same closely associated friends to provide the chief personnel for the reconstituted Elizabethan church. Elizabeth imprisoned the bishop of Chichester for charging Bill with heresy the Sunday following Bill's sermon at Paul's Cross, placed the bishop of Winchester under house arrest for his sermon at Mary's funeral, and sent bishops Watson and White to the Tower as an aftermath of the Westminster disputation. On Christmas Day she commanded the bishop of Carlisle to omit the elevation of the host and left the chapel when he refused to do so, repeating this insistence for the service at her coronation. Her proclamation of December 27, 1558, authorized the use of English for the epistle, the gospel, the Lord's Prayer, the

Creed, and the Litany. She is reported to have declared openly her satisfaction at the return of the exiles and to have desired Peter Martyr to take up once again his position at Oxford.[1] While there were moments of impatience during the course of the parliamentary session, few Protestants would have questioned Jewel's verdict that "we have a wise and religious queen, and one too who is favorably and propitiously disposed toward us."[2]

What were Elizabeth's own religious views? The one definite thing that can be said is that they can be ascertained only by inference, for Elizabeth never allowed anyone to peer into her heart and never fully disclosed her personal religious inclinations. Despite much ambiguity, the inferences that can be drawn are sufficiently persuasive to indicate the general thrust of Elizabeth's own religious sympathies.

In a superficial and purely negative sense, Elizabeth was made a Protestant by the circumstances of her birth. Even if a papal dispensation removed the consequences flowing from what Rome regarded as an illegitimate birth, still the taint would remain. On a more positive level, Elizabeth was born a Protestant by being her mother's daughter, for the Boleyn's were wedded to the Protestant interest and Elizabeth never forgot that she was the child of Anne Boleyn. Thomas Cranmer was her godfather, and Matthew Parker, whose mother's cousin had married Mary Boleyn, was her mother's chaplain. Only days before Anne Boleyn was sent to the Tower, she had charged Parker to look after the spiritual welfare of her infant daughter, a responsibility he honored as opportunity offered.

Perhaps none of this would have counted for much had it not been for Elizabeth's intense family loyalty. Given the sense of isolation and loneliness of her early years, it is not surprising that Elizabeth should have formed a strong attachment to her cousins as surviving members of her mother's family. Indications that she clung to her Boleyn ties are numerous. Elizabeth's closest confidante was Catherine Ashley, her governess under Edward, whose husband John Ashley was Elizabeth's cousin. Both John and his elder half-brother Richard were exiles under Mary, Richard Ashley having been a fellow of St. John's College, Cambridge. At her accession

1. *Zurich Letters, 1558–1579* (Cambridge, 1842), pp. 6, 11, 20, 44, 53–54, 55, 71–72; *Zurich Letters, 1558–1602*, Second series (Cambridge, 1845), p. 13.
2. *Zurich Letters, 1558–1579*, p. 33.

Elizabeth made John Ashley master of her jewel-house and a groom of the Privy Chamber. His wife Catherine became chief gentle-woman of the Privy Chamber (first lady of the ladies-in-waiting). The most prominent member of the court with a Boleyn connection was Francis Knollys, a leading Protestant and Marian exile, whose wife was one of Elizabeth's cousins. When the Knollys went into exile under Mary, Elizabeth had written a touching note to Catherine Knollys pledging her love and concern.

> Relieve your sorrow for your far journey with joy of your short return. And think this pilgrimage rather a proof of your friends than a leaving of your country. The length of time and distance of place separates not the love of friends. . . . When your need shall be most, you shall find my friendship greatest. Let others promise, and I will do, in words not more, in deeds as much. My power but small, my love as great as them whose gifts may tell their friendship's tale. . . . And to conclude, a word that hardly I can say I am driven by need to write—fare-well. It is which, in the sense one way, I wish; the other way, I grieve. Your loving cousin and ready friend.[3]

On their return, Elizabeth made Knollys her vice-chamberlain and a member of her council, while Catherine became a lady of her Privy Chamber. Another husband of a Boleyn cousin, Richard Sackville, was appointed under-treasurer and sworn to the Privy Council. Further evidence of Elizabeth's strong sense of attachment to her mother's family is provided by young Henry Carey, son of Mary Boleyn, who was first knighted and then created Baron Huns-don within two month's of Elizabeth's accession. Finally, Thomas Parry's step-son, John Fortescue, a more remote Boleyn connection, was made master of the wardrobe.

The influence exerted upon Elizabeth by the Protestantism of the Boleyn connection was reinforced by the religious sympathies of the circle surrounding Catherine Parr, Henry VIII's last wife. Catherine Parr was warmhearted, intelligent, well educated, and devoutly Protestant, as were most of those she chose as her ladies-in-waiting.[4] For Elizabeth the first happy period of her childhood

3. *Letters of Queen Elizabeth I*, ed. G. B. Harrison (London, 1968), p. 22.
4. Several of them, including Catherine herself, were suspected of ex-pressing sympathy and providing support for the "heretical" Anne Askew.

was when Catherine Parr brought her back to court, and her happiness within this circle must have given an emotional tone to whatever religious feelings she had.

Finally, Elizabeth was a Protestant by education. She was a child of the Protestantism which had nurtured young Edward and which she must have shared with those who were to constitute the central core of her supporters. The group, mostly from Cambridge, that supplied the initial personnel for her religious settlement was the same group that supplied the tutors and chaplains who shaped the minds and hearts of so many of her contemporaries, including a conspicuous number of notable and pious young women. William Grindal, her own tutor, was a convinced Protestant who had been brought by John Cheke from Cambridge. Moreover, Roger Ascham, who served as tutor after Grindal's death, was the author of a number of Protestant tractates, composed at the time he was tutoring Elizabeth. The stress of both men, as was true of their counterparts at court, was upon moral and religious as well as intellectual formation.[5] Not only were her tutors drawn from the ranks of the Athenians, they pursued with Elizabeth, as Cheke did with Edward, the same regime of studies which they had instituted at Cambridge. Elizabeth's inclusion of John Cheke's widow among her ladies-in-waiting suggests that she continued to identify herself with her tutors, for Mary Cheke had no connection, save friendship, which would commend her to Elizabeth for service in this capacity.

No one can tell how deeply Elizabeth was affected religiously by the convergence of these influences, but they do suggest that there is little likelihood that she looked back with nostalgia to any form of Henrician religion. Moreover, she was highly indignant at the treatment she had received at the hands of Roman Catholics. If she followed the example of her teachers and friends, she would have accepted as a minimum the results of the "new learning" and the importance of reforming the church in the light of a fuller understanding of the Scriptures and Christian antiquity. Beyond this one may reasonably speculate that Elizabeth would have found nothing

5. Cheke's practice followed by the others and reported by Ascham in *The Schoolmaster*, was to supplement the reading of Greek authors each morning with reading from the Greek New Testament, and to follow a similar procedure in Latin each afternoon with Melanchthon's *Loci communes* as supplementary reading. Cheke had been Ascham's tutor, and Ascham Grindal's.

offensive in the manifesto provided by John Jewel's "challenge sermon" preached at Paul's Cross, November 26, 1559, and preached again at Paul's Cross and at court in the spring of 1560. In the sermon Jewel challenged the papists to cite any authority that would indicate that there had been any private mass for 600 years after Christ, or communion in one kind, or prayers in a foreign tongue, or the bishop of Rome as the universal head of the whole church, or the doctrine of transubstantiation, or the elevation of the host of adoration, or any forbidding of people to read the Scriptures in their own tongue.[6]

Quite apart from any personal religious convictions, Elizabeth was reported to be "wonderfully afraid of allowing any innovations" except they be accomplished in due order "by authority and power of law." As Jewel subsequently put it, Elizabeth could not be "induced to effect . . . change without the sanction of law."[7] Elizabeth's preoccupation with the letter of the law was clearly in evidence during her first six or seven months as queen. A conspicuous expression of this preoccupation was the care with which she restricted changes in her own services of worship to that which was legally permissible. To help her at this point, Richard Goodrich apparently had been commissioned to prepare a memorandum at the beginning of her reign. Although Goodrich offered personal counsel with regard to practical political issues, the main thrust of his paper was to supply the new queen with legal advice about "divers points of religion."[8] After reviewing the past and identifying statutes that could be considered still in force, Goodrich concluded that as things stand "her majesty and all her subjects may by license of law use the English litany and suffrages used in King Henry's time, and besides her majesty in her closet may use the mass without lifting

6. Jewel's *Apology of the Church of England*, written anonymously early in 1561 at the request of Matthew Parker as a collective statement of the views of the English church, was a more formal exposition of the theological position of those most closely identified with Elizabeth's alteration of religion. It was written at the insistence of Nicholas Throckmorton in Paris who was convinced that France was ripe to embrace a moderate reformation and that they would respond to the pattern provided by the English settlement of religion. Jewel's *Apology* was translated into English by Cecil's sister-in-law, Ann (Cooke) Bacon, and her translation was commended in a prefatory note by Matthew Parker.

7. *Zurich Letters, 1558–1579*, pp. 10, 18.

8. For Goodrich's advice, see Gee, *The Elizabethan Prayer-book*, pp. 202–6.

up the host according to the ancient canons, and may also have at every mass some communicants with the ministers to be used in both kinds."

It was in keeping with Goodrich's legal advice that on Christmas day Elizabeth ordered the bishop of Carlisle to omit the elevation of the host in the royal chapel and felt free on Easter to have the litany and suffrages in English and to have the communion received in both kinds even though she had not given her assent to the supremacy bill which gave Parliament's authorization.[9] It is also interesting that, although the date when the revived and slightly modified 1552 prayer book was to be put into use was Midsummer Day, June 24, Elizabeth some six weeks earlier, immediately after giving her confirmation to the Act of Uniformity, began using the Edwardian prayer book as modified by Parliament in her own chapel. She had waited for its use to be legal but no longer.

Elizabeth's determination to keep religion firmly under the control of the crown very early became a consistent policy and remained so throughout her reign. She could not, however, disregard Parliament at the outset. The changes introduced by her father, brother, and sister all had been accomplished by acts of Parliament. Thus parliamentary action was required to undo what had been done as well as to establish firmly the legality of a further alteration of religion. Unwanted legislation needed to be repealed. Certain previously repealed acts needed to be revived and restored. A uniform order of common worship needed to be adopted. And legislation was needed restoring to her the royal supremacy enjoyed by her father touching or concerning all spiritual or ecclesiastical jurisdiction within her realms and dominions to the end that her power would be "the high-

9. Il Schifanoya relates that on Easter, Elizabeth appeared in her chapel "where mass was sung in English according to the use of her brother, King Edward, and the communion was received in both kinds, . . . nor did he wear anything but the mere surplice, having divested himself of the vestments in which he had sung mass," C.S.P., *Venetian, 1558–1580*, VII, 57. It is not surprising that Il Schifanoya missed some of the legal niceties of the service. It is true, of course, that a royal proclamation had been printed, in anticipation of the signing of the bill, authorizing communion in both kinds. This would have provided an excuse for others, but Elizabeth could rely on Goodrich's legal opinion. For an analysis placing greater stress on the importance of this occasion, see W. P. Haugaard, *Elizabeth and the English Reformation* (Cambridge, 1968), pp. 93–94.

est power under God to whom all men, within the same realms and dominions, by God's law [would] owe most loyalty and obedience afore and above all other powers."[10] Once these things were secured, Elizabeth's interest in parliamentary legislation for religion and the church was at an end. For the remainder of her reign she unwaveringly maintained that the government of the church fell within the royal prerogative.[11] She believed that, with the issuance of the Royal Injunctions in 1559, the alteration of religion had been completed. This was the settlement she sought to defend until the end of her life. John Jewel put Elizabeth's position succinctly when he wrote in 1566 that she is "unable to endure the least alteration in matters of religion."[12]

ESTRANGEMENT BETWEEN THE QUEEN AND HER CLERGY

A final feature of the religious settlement of 1559 was an estrangement between the queen and her chief clerical collaborators as the year drew to a close. While the estrangement was initially the prod-

10. The summary definition of royal authority is drawn from the first article of the 1559 Injunctions.

11. A rare exception when she authorized parliamentary action occurred as the result of the problem created when the Act of Uniformity abolished the existing rite for the consecration of bishops without reviving the rite adopted under Edward VI. Cecil struggled with the difficulty stemming from this oversight throughout the summer. It had not been resolved by October 5, 1559, when Cecil sent William Bill to Parker with a "determination" of some "good order" for consecrating bishops. "Things," he wrote, "be more untoward than I can suddenly rectify" (*Correspondence of Matthew Parker*, p. 78). Parliament was no longer sitting. Finally, it was agreed that Elizabeth, by her "supreme authority royal," should supply "whatever is or shall be lacking of those things which, by the statutes of this realm or by the laws of the church, are required or are necessary in this business." Signed opinions were secured from lawyers, both canonists and civilians, that Elizabeth's authorization was lawful and sufficient. Several years later, in response to a suit involving Edmund Bonner, a special act of Parliament was procured to confirm retroactively the legality of the consecrations. For a discussion of this point, see Philip Hughes, *The Reformation in England* (New York, 1954), III, 41–45. During the earlier period in 1559, Cecil was struggling with the problem of assembling a sufficient number of bishops to meet the requirement of the act of Henry VIII regulating episcopal appointments, which had been revived, for the consecration of Parker. He retained hope almost to the end that Tunstall would conform and participate.

12. *Zurich Letters, 1558–1579*, p. 149.

uct of a controversy over the presence of a small crucifix and two candles in the royal chapel, it is possible to speculate that temperament rather than conviction was involved in Elizabeth's stubborn defense of her "image" and "lights."

The issue of "ornaments" supposedly had been settled when further "order" had been taken by Elizabeth, "with the advice of her commissioners appointed . . . for causes ecclesiastical," in the form of Royal Injunctions to be enforced by those appointed by the queen for the visitation of the churches. There were some ambiguities in the Injunctions, and there were some irregularities both prior to and during the visitations. The required inventory of church goods had been misinterpreted by some as a listing of illicit articles to be destroyed,[13] although several of the items such as vestments and copes clearly were not illicit and one of the Articles of Inquiry stated explicitly that parishioners were to be admonished not to "sell, give, nor otherwise alienate any of their church goods." Still these irregularities were not the focal point of the controversy.

Elizabeth was away from London during August and September when, as the Spanish ambassador reported, the visitors took away "the crosses, images, and altars from St. Paul's and all the other London churches."[14] She returned from Kent and Surrey on September 28, 1559, for a wedding to be held in the royal chapel in Whitehall on October 5. The little silver cross and the two candles had been removed from the royal chapel, one may suppose as a result of the London visitation early in August. Elizabeth may not have noticed their absence on Sunday, October 1, but she made an issue of it at the wedding on Thursday. Still she let the wedding proceed. At evensong on Saturday, the crucifix and candles had been recovered and were back in place, "standing altar-wise," where they were to remain for the next few months as controversy swirled

13. Gee explains how this misunderstanding could occur. "Such inventories had a history. Under Edward they had often preceded the alienation of church goods. Those who read this injunction might naturally assume that this new inventory portended a similar surrender, and they would perceive that vestments, copes, and plate, which were enjoined by the 'ornaments rubric,' were placed by the Injunctions in the same category as those service-books which were rendered quite obsolete by the Uniformity Act," and presumably were to be destroyed as they had been under Edward VI. *The Elizabethan Prayer-book*, pp. 139–40, 190–94.

14. *C.S.P., Spanish, 1558–1567*, I, 89.

around them.[15] Henry Gee suggested that in the royal chapel Elizabeth was "at liberty to do as caprice or inclination directed."[16] Whether or not she was "at liberty" to violate her own Injunctions,[17] she was at least incensed and affronted that the change had been made in her absence and without her approval.

The sequence of events that followed is not clear, but at an early date Matthew Parker remonstrated with the queen, for on October 13, 1559, Francis Knollys wrote Parker wishing him "prosperity" in his "good enterprise against the enormities yet in the queen's closet retained (although without the queen's express commandment these toys were laid aside till now a late)" and committing Parker "and us all to the mighty protection of the living God." Knollys' reference to Parker's "good enterprise" may have been to an undated joint letter of Parker and others of "our brethren as now bear the office of bishop" setting forth at length "those authorities of the Scriptures, reasons, and pithy persuasions" which have persuaded them "to think and affirm images not expedient for the church of Christ." Being thus persuaded, this firm conviction will "not suffer us, without the great offending of God and grievous wounding of our own consciences (which God deliver us from), to consent to the erecting or retaining of the same in the place of worshipping." With our reasons against images in churches before you, "we trust and most earnestly ask it of God that they may also persuade your majesty, by your regal authority and in the zeal of God, utterly to remove this offensive evil out of the Church of England, to God's great glory and our own great comfort." By November 6, Parker reported to Cecil that "we" had been graciously received by the queen but "the principal cause not fully resolved." Since "the matter is in good towardness, we would wish we were called for again to continue our humble supplication to the finishment and stay of that offendicle, the more speed" the better, for "some fear danger is likely to arise thereof, as by letters, which this

15. For a report of the incident, see *C.S.P., Spanish, 1558–1567*, I, 105.
16. *Elizabethan Prayer-book*, p. 151.
17. Both the Injunctions and the Articles of Inquiry make it clear that images, candlesticks, and candles are to be destroyed, and the exception in the Edwardian Injunctions which permitted "two lights upon the high altar before the sacrament, which, for the signification that Christ is the very true light of the world, they shall suffer to remain still," was omitted. Gee, *The Elizabethan Clergy*, p. 48n.

morning I have sent to my lord of London at whose hands your worship may desire to have them, I perceive."[18]

Sometime during December Cox decided to take the bold step of virtually laying down an ultimatum. Being asked to preach in the royal chapel, Cox informed Elizabeth that he could not, "the lights and cross remaining." Angered by this tactic, Elizabeth asserted her authority, and in the end, after "a great while," Cox's resistance crumbled and by December 21 he consented, as he put it, only with a "trembling conscience" to appear once again in the chapel. With a strange lack of tact, he insisted upon writing a letter to the queen to make clear his position and to support his initial refusal. He did not wish to judge her, and "therefore I was content, albeit, God he knoweth, with a trembling conscience, to minister and communicate, as appeareth, upon this great and weighty consideration. Bear with me, most gracious sovereign. For the tender mercy of God, force not my conscience so sore."[19]

The controversy continued to boil, as indicated by Sampson's letter to Peter Martyr on January 6, 1560. "The altars indeed are removed and images also throughout the kingdom; the crucifix and candles are retained at court alone. And the wretched multitude ... will imitate it of their own accord."[20] On February 4, Jewel wrote Martyr that the issue was finally to be fully joined and resolved.

> This controversy about the crucifix is now at its height. . . .
> A disputation on the subject will take place tomorrow. The
> moderators will be persons selected by the council. The dis-
> putants on the one side are the archbishop of Canterbury and
> Cox, and on the other Grindal, the bishop of London, and
> myself. The decision rests with the judges [presumably Robert

18. *Correspondence of Matthew Parker*, pp. 79–95, 97, 105. In addition to Parker, the "bishops" sending the joint letter were probably Grindal, Cox, Sandys, Scory, Barlow, and perhaps Meyrick. Only Scory and Barlow had been consecrated, but the others were functioning as "bishops, elect."

19. John Strype, *Annals of the Reformation* (Oxford, 1824), I, i, 260. Cox's letter of justification is printed in ibid., I, ii, 500–503. After his surrender, Cox reported to Peter Martyr: "By the blessing of God all those heads of religion are restored to us which we maintained in the time of King Edward. We are only constrained, to our great distress of mind, to tolerate in our churches the image of the cross and him who was crucified. The Lord must be entreated that this stumbling-block may at length be removed." *Zurich Letters, 1558–1579*, p. 66.

20. *Zurich Letters, 1558–1579*, p. 63.

Catlyne, lord chief justice of the Court of Queen's Bench, and James Dyer, chief justice of the Court of Common Pleas[21]]. I smile, however, when I think with what grave and solid reasons they [Parker and Cox] will defend their little cross. Whatever be the result, I will write to you more at length when the disputation is over; yet, as far as I can conjecture, I shall not again write to you as a bishop. For matters are come to that pass that either the crosses of silver and tin, which we everywhere have broken in pieces, must be restored or our bishoprics relinquished.[22]

A month later, on March 4, 1560, Cox reported that, while difference of opinion continues to exist "with respect to setting up the crucifix in churches," the issue had officially been resolved and "we are in that state that no crucifix is now-a-days to be seen in any of our churches."[23] Sandys added, in a letter to Peter Martyr, "only the popish vestments remain in our church, I mean the copes; which, however, we hope will not last very long."[24]

One can only speculate as to what had taken place. Usually it is simply said that a compromise was reached. Apparently what had occurred was that Elizabeth was persuaded to submit the whole question of ornaments to legal determination, to an interpretation of her own Injunctions and whatever statutes had a bearing upon

21. The two chief justices were commonly referred to as "the judges." It was appropriate for them to be called upon to interpret the law. But, in this instance, it was doubly appropriate for they were singularly qualified to serve in a face-saving enterprise as impartial interpreters. Both had been Marian appointees, and neither one had a Cambridge or a Gray's Inn connection. In terms of religion, they had no strong commitments.

22. Ibid., pp. 67–68. Sandys reviewing the controversy on April 1, 1560, wrote that he too "was very near being deposed from my office," having been "rather vehement in this matter" and "incurring the displeasure of the queen," ibid., p. 74. It is likely that Grindal had this heated controversy partially in mind when more than six and a half years later, in the midst of the dispute over vestments, he wrote: "We, who are now bishops, on our first return and before we entered on our ministry, contended long and earnestly for the removal of those things that have occasioned the present dispute. But as we were unable to prevail, either with the queen or the Parliament, we judged it best, after a consultation on the subject, not to desert our churches for the sake of a few ceremonies, and those not unlawful in themselves, especially since the pure doctrine of the gospel remained in all its integrity and freedom." Ibid., p. 169.

23. Zurich Letters, 1558–1602, Second series, pp. 41–42.

24. Zurich Letters, 1558–1579, p. 74.

them. Parker and Cox had taken a less unyielding stance in the crunch, but they were scarcely calculated to be effective adversaries to whatever arguments were put forward by Grindal and Jewel in the disputation. The verdict was a compromise of sorts. The crucifix and the candles were ruled to have been banned by the Injunctions, and permissible clerical vestments for public worship were ruled to have been governed by the general directive concerning clerical dress. This restricted vestments to those used in the last year of Edward VI, i.e., the cope and the surplice, instead of those permissible under the "ornaments rubric" had it not been modified by the Injunctions.

Elizabeth accepted the decision, with outward grace perhaps, but not without inward irritation and resentment. She had been given a face-saving device to escape a stalemate, yet it was not a capitulation for she was careful to remind Parker that she had legal ground, conferred upon her by the "ornaments proviso" to issue new injunctions and directives without any further parliamentary sanction.[25] Moreover, from this time forward she was to exhibit a persistent dislike of the clergy, expressing her resentment against them often in petty and capricious forms of harassment as opportunity arose, and taking vicarious delight in forcing Archbishop Parker, with his "Advertisements" of 1566, to stand alone without her public support in enforcing the code of clerical dress prescribed in the 1559 Injunctions, as interpreted by "the judges" in 1560. In a letter to Cecil, Parker confessed his own shock, discomfort, and discouragement in being verbally abused by the queen to such an extent that she "expressed to me a repentance" that her bishops had been "appointed in office, wishing it had been otherwise."[26] In this game of tit for tat, one could never know from what direction to expect the ire of the queen to be aroused, as Alexander Nowell disconcertingly discovered in March, 1561.

Nowell was preaching at St. Paul's, whither the queen frequently resorted. It was New Year's Day according to the old calendar.

25. *Correspondence of Matthew Parker*, pp. 132, 157.
26. Ibid., p. 157. Much of Elizabeth's ill-pleasure found expression in a growing antipathy to a married clergy (ibid., p. 148). For comments concerning Mandell Creighton's appraisal of Elizabeth's temperamental behavior and the problems it created for those who sought to serve her, see G. R. Elton, *Studies in Tudor and Stuart Politics and Government* (Cambridge, 1974), I, 241.

Earlier Nowell had secured several fine woodcuts and pictures from abroad representing the stories of the saints and martyrs. He had them placed opposite the epistles and gospels of their festivals in a prayer book, and had the book richly bound. He then laid it on the cushion for the queen's use in the place where she customarily sat. He intended it as a New Year's gift and thought that it would please the queen. It had the opposite effect. When she came to her place, she found the book. She opened it, perused it, frowned, and then reddened and closed it. She summoned the verger, and asked him to bring her the old book which had been replaced.

After the sermon, Elizabeth went to the dean in his vestry and inquired how the new book came to be on her cushion. Nowell replied that he had placed it there. She asked why he has done so, and he replied that it was a New Year's gift. "You could never present me with worse," she responded. "You know I have an aversion to idolatry: to images and pictures of this kind." When Nowell asked wherein was the idolatry, Elizabeth said: "In the cuts resembling angels and saints; nay, grosser absurdities—pictures resembling the blessed Trinity." Nowell confessed that he had meant no harm. "You must needs be ignorant then," responded Elizabeth. "Have you forgot our proclamation against images, pictures, and Romish relics in the churches? . . . Pray let no more of these mistakes, or of this kind, be committed within the churches of our realm for the future."[27]

The story undoubtedly was embellished in the telling of it, but Elizabeth's resentment at anyone having the temerity to tamper with her own copy of the prayer book is strikingly reminiscent of her irritation with those who removed the little crucifix and candles in her chapel without her knowledge and while she was absent. Since she earlier had expressed her irritation impetuously and had been forced to back down, she must have taken almost diabolical pleasure in being able to call Nowell to account for having, as she saw it, violated the same Injunction.

ELIZABETH'S AUTHORITY LEFT OPEN-ENDED

What may one say of the religious settlement of 1559 as represented by the Act of Supremacy and the Act of Uniformity as completed by the Injunctions?

27. Strype, *Annals*, I, i, 408–10.

There was much consultation among the coterie of "friends," both lay and clerical, who were most closely involved in effecting the settlement. While all had parts to play, the control of timing and strategy was retained by the government throughout. For the government, one may read Elizabeth, Cecil, and members of the Privy Council. A more realistic assessment would be to regard government policy as being initiated and directed by Cecil with the full acquiescence of the queen.

In this process there is no reason to believe that Elizabeth was ignorant of the issues. Whatever her views, she was not theologically illiterate. John Hooper, who was a court preacher at the time, may have overstated the case in 1550 when he wrote to Bullinger of both young King Edward and his sister Elizabeth. After informing the Zurich reformer of the theologically informed religious enthusiasm of twelve year old Edward, Hooper continued: "The daughter of the late king by Queen Anne is inflamed by the same zeal for the religion of Christ. She not only knows what true religion is, but has acquired such proficiency in Greek and Latin that she is able to defend it by the most just arguments . . . so that she encounters few adversaries whom she does not overcome."[28] This was hyperbole, but it does recall the regime of study to which she had been subjected. If young Edward, Lady Jane Grey, Anthony Cooke's daughters, and others who received much the same education as Elizabeth exhibited a surprising degree of theological sophistication, there is little cause to believe that Elizabeth was any less well informed. She may have lacked the depth of religious conviction of some of the others, but it was not for want of knowledge.

When Elizabeth came to the throne, delicate maneuvers and changes of pace were necessary to carry out the alteration of religion in such a way that the desired reforms would be brought to a successful conclusion. Since the reasons for the strategy pursued at any given moment could not always be fully disclosed, there were intermittent periods of impatience, consternation, and dismay among those who were not always consulted with regard to details of timing and strategy and who therefore had to be content with hints of reassurance. As one traces the fluctuating mood revealed in the letters of the "friends" among the clergy, one notes that the

28. *Original Letters Relative to the English Reformation* (Cambridge, 1846), I, 76.

periods of despondency were followed by more optimistic reports and then by a prevailing conviction that all was well once the visitations began.

The striking feature of Elizabeth's first eleven months as queen is the lack of solid evidence that she was out of sympathy or in any way out of step with those closest to her who were helping fashion the religious settlement. It seems clear that her assignment was to play for time. This she did quite flawlessly in spite of her known past affinity for those of Protestant persuasion. Until peace with France was secured, she was evasive in her interviews with the Spanish and Mantuan representatives, "dissembled" her religious views, and did not close the door to the possibility of a Spanish marriage. When news was received that the peace negotiations had produced an acceptable treaty, there was a change of front. Elizabeth appears to have experienced a great sense of relief and release in being able to announce to the Spanish ambassador that she was a "heretic" and could not marry the Spanish king.

Prior to March 19 when word of the treaty reached London, Elizabeth had displayed no outward displeasure with those selected to preach in her presence, either in her chapel or on public occasions such as the opening of Parliament. A similar outward harmony continued to prevail thereafter. She raised no objection to those chosen for the post-Easter preaching assignments. She accepted the prayer book with no outward question, and offered no dissent to Grindal's presentation of it to the public. She gave no indication of finding fault with the Injunctions which were issued in her name and by her authority in accordance with the "proviso" of the Act of Uniformity. In retrospect, it seems surprising that Elizabeth viewed with equanimity the widespread and widely publicized destruction of "ornaments" during August and September in London and throughout the country as a result of the visitations being carried out in her name and by her authority. Although Elizabeth was out of London, the court was never so isolated as to be unaware of what was taking place in other parts of the realm. Yet there was no word of condemnation, no effort to put a stop to the spectacle in many parishes of church goods being publicly burned.

The first fatal mistake for those concerned with getting rid of "the scenic apparatus of divine worship" had occurred when someone, presumably during the visitation of London, removed the crucifix and candles from the royal chapel without Elizabeth's knowledge. This she regarded as an affront to her dignity and position. She was not subject to visitation; she was carrying out the visitation. The second fatal mistake was to make a public issue of the incident instead of letting Cecil resolve the matter privately. Cox's refusal to preach in the chapel as long as the cross and lights remained made matters worse, and was compounded by the attempts of other bishops to coerce the queen by threats of resignation. Probably what angered Elizabeth most, turning irritation and resentment into unyielding stubbornness, was the virtual ultimatum presented by Parker, in a letter on behalf of all the bishops, giving "reasons" for the removal of such images from all places of worship. This was the most direct challenge of all to Elizabeth's own conception of herself as "supreme governor" of the Church of England, for it was a corporate act and thus tinged with official character. The implication was the existence of an independent authority within the church.

An end to the stalemate was finally negotiated, presumably by Cecil, but the damage had been done. As a result of the dispute, Elizabeth became alienated from the clergy in general and the bishops in particular. Henceforth she frequently treated them with the contempt she believed they deserved, and seldom missed an opportunity to remind them of their proper place within the ordered realm of England. The issue of vestments had not been satisfactorily resolved, for few of the bishops were prepared to give the "compromise" at this point the stringent enforcement that the author of the "Device for the alteration of religion" believed to be necessary to nip in the bud future dissent and agitation.

A final and perhaps unintended consequence of the ornaments proviso was to leave the queen's authority in a broad area of religious practice open-ended. Although Elizabeth was later to say that she would not have signed the Act of Uniformity without the ornaments proviso, it is not clear that at the time she was fully aware of the potential power being conferred. Much more likely this was a discovery after the event. What one would guess was in everyone's mind at the time was simply a single taking of further "order" to bring the settlement to completion. Few could have realized that it made her, in most areas of controversy, fully independent of Parliament, convocation, and the bishops.

IX. AFTERWORD

A conspicuous feature of the Elizabethan regime at its outset was the harmony which prevailed between the queen, the council, the Commons, and the forces of Protestant reform represented by what has been described as the Cambridge connection. William Paulet, marquis of Winchester and lord treasurer, was the only active promoter of disaffection on the council but his voice was muted and his influence circumscribed. In spite of the confusion and delay in reaching a religious settlement occasioned by a recalcitrant house of lords and by disconcerting changes of signals in the lower house, for almost a year after Elizabeth's accession there were few signs of any fundamental disagreement between the queen and those who constituted the core of her support. The path being pursued meandered at times, and the road ahead was not always clear even to some of the most deeply involved participants, but their recurring apprehension was repeatedly dissipated by reassuring action. This harmony, however, was not to continue. On several fronts there was to be tension over a variety of issues and a jockeying for position.

The first break in the general harmony of aim and intention, as has been noted, came in the closing months of 1559 over the issue of the crucifix and candles in the royal chapel. Although papered over by the decision of "the judges" in February 1560, the rift between Elizabeth and her bishops was to remain. Moreover, Elizabeth's subsequent intervention in 1565 to insist that the provision in the Injunctions with regard to clerical dress be observed and enforced with uncompromising severity widened the rift and introduced a painful division among those who were in substantial agreement on almost all points of religious faith. The bishops were thrown into some disarray and a line of division increasingly separated the bishops from the more zealous of the lower clergy and of the laity.

Grindal and Horne spoke for almost all the bishops when they explained that they disliked the vestments as much as anyone else, but, having been reassured by Martyr and Bullinger that the offensive garments were tolerable in the existing situation, they were prepared to regard the vestments as things indifferent which the queen had a right to impose for order's sake. The bishops had been badly burned in their first confrontation with the queen, and they were hesitant to defy her once again. Parker and Cox, who had taken the lead in opposing what was called the "offendicle" in the royal chapel, had felt at firsthand the lash of royal anger. This may have made them more hesitant than the others to risk all that had been gained by engaging in another encounter with the queen. Most of the bishops were somewhat ambivalent. They were willing to adjust personally to the queen's demands, but they were slow to move with vigor in testing the consciences of others. Even Parker had little stomach for the enterprise until, after being goaded repeatedly by Elizabeth, he became irritated by the lack of sympathy he found among those who failed to appreciate his dilemma.

The subsequent story of the consequences of Elizabeth's spasmodic interventions in church affairs and of her unyielding resistance to any initiative for further reform being taken by Parliament is familiar. It has been reconstructed with clarity, discrimination, and attention to its varied nuances in Patrick Collinson's *The Elizabethan Puritan Movement*. The issue of vestments was followed by controversy over "prophesyings," "fast days," and other means of independent action within the parishes. In all these issues which were to trouble the English church for an indefinite future the fundamental question was, in the words of Collinson, "whether the queen in all circumstances was to be obeyed." Few of the bishops were ready to answer that question wholeheartedly in the affirmative, and varying degrees of laxity prevailed in different dioceses. On the other hand, whatever their sympathies may have been, "the bishops rarely refused to execute royal policy where the necessity was unavoidable." Only Grindal, late in his career when he was archbishop of Canterbury, "ever dared explain to the queen's face that as a bishop of Christ's church he was subject to a higher power, and the result [of his forthrightness] was suspension from office and the irretrievable loss of her favor."[1]

The second break in the general harmony pervading the early Elizabethan government came with the emergence of Robert Dudley, master of the horse, as the queen's "favorite." Dudley comes

1. Patrick Collinson, *The Elizabethan Puritan Movement* (Berkeley, 1967), p. 60.

148

on the scene as a central figure during the summer of 1560 just at the close of this study. Prior to this he had cut a modest figure at court, keeping in the background and avoiding political entanglements. This changed with his new relationship to the queen. As her "favorite" Dudley had a disintegrating effect on court politics, for he had the queen's ear and rapidly became a rival center of influence in the government, informally at first and then formally as a member of the council. It was not until 1564 that Dudley finally recognized that the prize of marriage and a crown was to be beyond his grasp. He continued, nevertheless, to pursue policies of his own and to foster an independent base of support.

The dozen years following the emergence of Dudley as the queen's "favorite" have been described by Wallace MacCaffrey as the "testing-time" when it was to be determined whether or not Elizabeth's government could achieve sufficient stability to survive. Dudley's activities during this period cost Cecil a large portion of the initiative he had been able to exercise by forcing him to spend much of his time countering Dudley's moves. Moreover, the cohesion among Cecil's friends was impaired by the patronage Dudley extended after 1561 to the more impatient Protestants and by Dudley's willingness to undertake more daring initiatives. Throckmorton was a major defector, being attracted by Dudley's less cautious style and becoming perhaps Dudley's political mentor and chief strategist. The alignment of those within the council tended to vary from issue to issue. The shifting balance of influence continued throughout the 1560's, and was not brought to an end until 1571 or 1572 when Elizabeth resolved the ambiguity by making it clear that Cecil was to be her chief minister and advisor. By this time the old issues which had divided Cecil and Dudley had been reduced to differences of means; not ends. A modus vivendi was reached acceptable to Dudley, which allowed them to work together within broad areas of common concern. Cecil's preeminence in the council and affairs of state was confirmed without Dudley's being displaced at court as the queen's "favorite."

The story of this "testing-time," with its interplay between Elizabeth, Cecil, and Dudley, has been brilliantly told in fascinating detail and with persuasive insight by Wallace MacCaffrey in *The Shaping of the Elizabethan Regime*. There is nothing of importance to add to his account, for the reader will readily note the ways in which the type of activity and influence represented by the Cambridge connection contributed to what MacCaffrey described as a slow turn from a royalty-centered domain, "paternalistic and dynastic in outlook," to a state in which "the magnetic pole of politics would not quite coincide with that visible and apparent center of attraction, the throne." The English national interest was beginning to be distinguished from that of the sovereign. Slowly but surely "the traditional view that the great decisions of state were solely the business of the crown was being shunted firmly aside." The immediate result was "a hybrid political order . . . accommodating in uneasy partnership a still potent monarchy and an as yet ill-defined political elite"—an elite "which, while loyal to the crown, drew its strength from sources quite independent of the monarchy."[2]

2. Wallace MacCaffrey, *The Shaping of the Elizabethan Regime* (Princeton, 1968), pp. 4-5, 15-17, 452, 471, 479-83.

INDEX

Bullingham, Nicholas, 41n, 105
Butts, William, 7, 27n, 36; at Cambridge, 48; and Cheke and Smith, 50–53; and Cranmer and Denny, 51n; and Edward's tutor, 73–75

Calvin, John, 98
Cambridge connection, 3–7, 39, 144, 150
——defined, 7, 29–30, 35–38, 41–42, 118n
——dominance at Cambridge, 3, 53–54, 56–59
——Elizabeth's government, predominance in, 39–40
——key figures: Butts, 7, 52–53, 73–78; Cecil, 77; Cheke, 53–54
——members: at Cambridge, 54–56, 86; London connections, 4, 27n, 35, 37n, 77
——relationships, personal and family, 27, 28, 35, 37, 41, 63, 64n, 65, 66, 82 84n
——religious settlement, 40, 99–105
Cambridge University: center of influence, 45–46; chief ministers of king as chancellors, 46; intellectual and religious ferment, 46–49; means of upward mobility, 39–40, 46–47, 61, 63–64; officers, 52, 53, 56; Royal Injunctions of 1535, 49; Smith and Cheke as luminaries, 3, 49–50; student relationships, 41, 54n
Carey, Henry, 133
Carr, Nicholas, 54
Catlyne, Robert, 140–41
Cave, Ambrose, 18, 20, 27, 117; and Cecil, 22–23; at Cambridge, 55n
Cecil, William, 4, 5, 6, 36, 55n, 78–79, 95–96, 137n, 139, 142, 146, 149
——education: at Cambridge, 41, 46; pupil of Cheke, 54, 62–63; Greek scholar, 5, 63; at St. John's, 62–63
——London, early activities in, 62–68; Gray's Inn, 38, 64, 68, 82–86
——political activity: Cambridge connection, 77; Elizabeth, principal secretary for, 10–11, 19–21, 26–28, 32–33, 105–9, 148–49; in Northumberland's service, 77, 84–85; parliamentary strategy and control of House of Commons, 118, 119; personnel recruitment, 107n; in Somerset's service, 83–84
——relationships, 27–29; Elizabeth, 6, 9–18, 31–33, 86; family connections, 27n, 63, 63n; marries Cheke's sister, 63–64; marries Mildred Cooke, 64, 82; Walter Mildmay, 28n; Catherine Parr, 13–14, 83; William Parr, 27; Thomas Parry, 13–14; Francis Russell, 27; Thomas Smith, 78; Nicholas Throckmorton, 11, 13, 22–24, 31–32; Catherine Willoughby, 15; women, 7, 14–15, 64–65
——religion: bishops' reports, 109n; involvements, 85, 99–105; views, 95, 101n; visitation of Cambridge, 104
Chaloner, Thomas, 27n, 29, 66–67, 78, 79, 81; at St. John's, 54
Cheke, John, 3, 4, 27n, 28, 36, 58, 58n, 79
——Cambridge, 49–56: child of university, 51–52; Greek pronunciation, 43–44; influence, 41, 53–54, 56; provost of King's, 56; public orator, 51n; regius professor, 53; at St. John's, 54; students, 54–55; teaching methods, 36, 55, 134

——London: ecclesiastical laws, 84–85; exile and arrest, 20, 87; Gray's Inn, 68n; Lord's Supper, conference on, 85; principal secretary, 87; tutor to Edward, 69–70, 73–75, 77

——relationships, 51–52, 54–55: Bucer, 59–60; Butts, 52–53; 73–78; Cecil, 62–64; Parker, 55–56; Smith, 49–50, 53

Cheke, Mary, 63–64, 134

Cheke, Peter, 51–52

Cheyney, Richard, 105n; at Cambridge, 55

Cheyney, Thomas, 18n, 20

"Civil service," incipient development of, 7, 81

Clinton, Edward Fiennes de, 18, 19

Cole, Thomas, 87; at Cambridge, 86

Colet, John, 47

Collinson, Patrick, 8, 148

Commissions, overlapping memberships of, 84–85

Cooke, Anthony, 6, 26, 27n, 64, 79n, 85, 117; Athenians, links with, 118n; daughters, 64n, 144; family connections, 37n; government position, failure to secure, 107n; in House of Commons, 118n; tutor to Edward, 69

Cordell, William, 20

Cox, Richard, 40, 55, 102, 118n, 148; benefices, 87; at Cambridge, 49, 87; daughter marries Parker's son, 38n; Ecclesiastical Commission, 104; Elizabeth, ultimatum to, 140–42; initial episcopal appointee, 104; exile, 6; Lenten sermon, 103; Parliament, sermon at opening, 103, 114, 131; "royal nursery," dean of, 69; 'Spital sermon, 103, 122; visitation commissioner, 129; Westminster disputation, 103, 122n

Cranmer, Thomas, 7, 25, 27, 36, 45, 59, 66, 68, 69, 73, 74, 75, 76, 113, 132; at Cambridge, 46, 48n; chaplains of, 87

Cromwell, Thomas, 26, 44, 45–46, 66, 74, 81, 82

Davies, Richard, 104

Day, George, 55

Denny, Anthony, 7, 17, 27n, 36, 65, 67n, 73, 75, 76, 79n; Butts, collaboration with, 73; Cambridge connection, 40; family connections, 37n

Denny, Joyce, 65

Dering, Edward, 100

"Device for alteration of religion," 111–14, 146

Doctor's Commons, 67

Downham, William, 105

Dudley, Ambrose, 21, 22

Dudley, John, duke of Northumberland, 15, 76, 77n, 84

Dudley, Robert, 20, 21, 22, 32, 100–101, 105n, 148–49

Dyer, James, 141

Edward VI, 3, 7, 15, 144; accession, 75; chaplains, 87; education, 62, 68–70

Elizabeth

——education, 70–71: Cambridge regime, 134; knowledge of Greek, 5, 36; tutors, 70

——reign: accession, 9–11, 90; bills of supremacy and uniformity, 124; Commons, relationship with, 4–5; government, character of, 25, 61; legal procedures, 135, 136

——relationships: Boleyn loyalty, 26, 132–33; Cecil, 6, 9–18, 31–33, 149; Robert Dudley, 23, 32–33, 148–49; Catherine Knollys, 133; Catherine Parr, 15–17, 68; religious leadership, 4–5, 137–43; Thomas Seymour, 17–20

——religion: crucifix and candles controversy, 138–42; married clergy, 128–29; 142n; "ornaments," 142, 145; 1552 prayer book, 94–95, 136, 145; privy councillors constituted interim ecclesiastical commissioners, 126; Royal Injunctions of 1559, 137; royal prerogative, 131, 132–33, 143, 146, 148; views, 90, 91–92, 97, 124n, 131–37, 144, 145

Episcopal appointments, 40–41, 87–88, 104–5, 105n

Erasmian pronunciation of Greek, 3

Erasmus, 43, 47, 57–58

"Establishment," 29–30, 144

——defined, 34–35: described as "friends," 118n

——relationships at Cambridge, 41; Cambridge personnel in church, 40–41; Cambridge personnel in government, 39, 77n; family relationships, 27, 28, 28n, 63, 64n, 65, 66, 82; friendships, illustrated, 37, 84n; Gray's Inn, 38; membership on commissions, 84–85

Fairlie, Henry, 34–35

Family relationships, 27, 28, 37n, 63, 64n, 65, 66, 82, 132–33

Feckenham, John, 84, 123n

Feudal society, shift from vertical relationships of, 7, 35, 150

Fisher, John, 47

Fitzalen, Henry, 18, 19, 31

Fitzwilliam, William, 21

Foreman, Thomas, 48

Fortescue, John, 133

France, peace with, 20, 24, 32, 92, 115, 121, 121–22, 144

Frankfort, troubles at, 6

Frith, John, 48

Gardiner, Stephen, 3, 20, 21, 35, 61, 68, 75n, 83, 85; at Cambridge, 46; ebbing of authority, 57n; Greek pronunciation, 43–45

Gerard, Gilbert, 20, 28, 36, 80–81; at Cambridge, 55n

Goodrich, Richard, 29, 78, 80, 135–36; at Cambridge, 55n; religious settlement, 110–11

Goodrich, Thomas, 67

Gray's Inn, 29n, 38, 64, 65, 66, 68n, 80, 81; Cambridge link, 67, 68n; members in government, 38–39; role of, 67

Greek, controversy over pronunciation, 43–45, 50

Gresham, Thomas, 19, 28, 36, 66, 80; at Cambridge, 55n; family connections, 37, 66

Grey, Henry, 70

Grey, Lady Jane, 70, 71, 144

Grindal, Edmund, 6, 11n, 40, 85, 88, 115, 140n, 147
——relationships: Bucer, 59; at Cambridge, 86; Cecil, 107; chaplain to Edward VI, 87; Elizabeth, 148
——religious settlement, 102; cross and candles disputation, 140–41; Ecclesiastical Commission member, 103–4; initial episcopal appointee, 104; Lenten sermon, 103; prayer book proclamation at Paul's Cross, 103, 131; Westminster disputation, 103, 122n
Grindal, William, 4, 134; at St. John's, 54; tutor to Elizabeth, 13, 70
Guest, Edmund, 103, 105n, 122n; at Cambridge 55; letter misdated by Strype, 95–96

Haddon, James, 4, 71; at King's College, Cambridge, 55n
Haddon, Walter, 19, 25, 28, 36, 87, 104; and Bucer, 59; at Cambridge, 53, 55; Cheke, 54; master of Trinity Hall, 57; public orator, 51n
Hastings, Henry, 21, 22
Heath, Nicholas, 10n, 12–13, 18, 116, 122, 123n
Henry VIII, 7, 68, 72–75, 76
Herbert, William, 18, 33, 71, 76, 82; and Parr, 27
Heynes, Simon, 49
Hoby, Philip, 29n, 82n; friend of Cecil and Mildmay, 37n
Hoby, Thomas, 29, 37n, 38n, 82n; at St. John's, 54n
Hooper, John, 144
Horizontal relations of post-feudal society, 7, 35, 150
Horne, Robert, 85, 102, 147; chaplain to Edward VI, 87; Durham nomination, 88; episcopal appointment delayed, 105; at St. John's, 54; sermon at Paul's Cross, 103; 'Spital sermon, 103, 122; visitation commissioner, 104; visitation of Cambridge, 104; Westminster disputation, 103, 122n
Howard, William, of Effingham, 19, 20

Inns of Court, 38–39

Jewel, John, 7, 40–41, 94–95, 102, 132, 137; *Apology for the Church of England*, 135n; "challenge sermon," 135; initial episcopal appointee, 104; reports to Peter Martyr, 113–14, 121, 123, 124–25, 140–42; visitation commissioner, 104, 129; Westminster disputation, 103, 122n
Jones, Norman, x

Kelke, Roger, at St. John's, 54
Killigrew, Henry, 37n, 40n, 82n
Kitchin, Anthony, 116, 126
Knollys, Catherine, 133
Knollys, Francis, 6, 19, 25, 27, 36, 85, 99, 117, 118, 133, 139
Knox, John, 30–31

Latimer, Hugh, 48, 72; at Cambridge, 48
Latimer, William, at Cambridge, 55
Laymen, in government, 61, 76

Lever, Thomas, 114n, 129; at St. John's, then master, 54, 57
Lord's Supper, conference on, 85

MacCaffrey, Wallace, 8, 26, 29–30, 34, 35, 41, 149
Madew, John, 57; at St. John's, 54, 86
Manners, Henry, 85
Marian exile, obscures relationships, 5–6
Martyr, Peter, 25, 40, 87, 88, 98, 102, 103, 132, 140, 147; influence of, 58, 60
Mary Tudor, queen of England, 9, 11, 12, 15, 16, 20, 58
Mason, John, 10n, 14, 18, 19, 20, 28, 31, 37n, 61, 81, 115
May, William, 40, 55, 102; at Cambridge, 49; Queens' College president, 56;
   on Ecclesiastical Commission, 104; and Edward VI, 86–87; Gray's Inn,
   68n; visitation of Cambridge, 104; archbishop of York nominee, 104
Melville, James, 31
Mildmay, Walter, 4, 19, 25, 27n, 28, 36, 65–66, 117; at Cambridge, 55; Court
   of Augmentations, 79–80; family connections, 37n; founder of Emmanu-
   el College, 99; Gray's Inn, 4, 68n; marries Mary Walsingham, 65
More, Thomas, 47, 61
Morice, Ralph, 73
Morison, Richard, 27n, 28, 38n, 79, 81, 82n

Neale, J. E., 94, 95n, 97, 99, 112n, 119n, 120n
Needham, Paul, ix–x, 51n
Norfolk, representation at Cambridge, 48n
Nowell, Alexander, 104; Gray's Inn, 68n; Elizabeth's prayer book, 142–43
Nowell, Lawrence, 87; at Cambridge, 55

Oglethorpe, Owen, 122n, 131, 136
Ornaments proviso, 98–99, 124; rubric modified by Injunctions, 138; ruling
   of "the judges," 141–42
Oxford University, 40, 47, 61, 72, 87, 105

Paget, William, 20–21, 58n, 61, 75, 81
Parker, Matthew, 6, 40, 49, 56, 96, 125, 129, 137n, 148
——Cambridge, 46, 48; Corpus Christi, master of, 2, 56; vice-chancellor, 56
——relationships, 38n; Bacon, 66; Anne Boleyn, 132; Bucer, 59; Cecil, 63n,
   106–7, 142; Cheke, 55–56
——religious settlement, 102; archbishopric of Canterbury, 106–7; clerical
   dress, harrassment by Elizabeth, 142; cross and candles controversy, 139,
   146; Ecclesiastical Commission, 103–4; Lenten sermon, 103, 131; Paul's
   Cross sermon, 103, 122
Parkhurst, John, 40, 41n, 72, 105
Parliament: control of House of Commons, 116–17, 118; supremacy and uniformity bills, passage of, 123–24; tactics, 115–16, 119, 121–25
Parr, Anne, 70, 71
Parr, Catherine, 27n, 62, 68–69, 71–72, 82, 133–34; education, 71; and Cecil,
   13, 15; and Elizabeth, 15–17; and Catherine Willoughby, 71–72

Scory, John, 40, 103, 104, 122n; at Cambridge, 40
Scotland, 24, 30–32
Seckford, Thomas, 19, 28; at Cambridge, 40
Seton, Alexander, 72
Seymour, Edward, Lord Protector, 15, 17, 20, 62, 64; and Edward's accession, 75; loss of power to Dudley, 85
Seymour, Jane, 71
Seymour, Thomas, 14, 16, 17–18, 20, 21, 71, 77n, 83
Sidney, Henry, 21, 22
Smith, Thomas, 3, 26n 29, 36, 58, 79, 82n, 117; at Cambridge, 49–51, 53; and Cheke, 50, 53; Greek pronunciation, 43; public orator, 51; rapid advance at court, 77–78; regius professor, 53; status under Northumberland and Elizabeth, 78; vice-chancellor, 56
Spanish ambassador, estimate of Cecil, 18, 99
Stafford, George, 48
Stone, Lawrence, 39
Strassburg, 6, 101; importance of, 58–60, 88

Throckmorton, Nicholas, 11, 22, 25n, 36, 78–79, 82, 85, 99, 110; and Cecil, 11, 13, 22–24, 31–32; and Cecil's son, 23n; defection, 149; French embassy, 24; Jewel's *Apology*, 135n; and Parrs, 22
Thynne, John, 37n, 66n, 117
Tonge, Roger, at Cambridge, 87
Tunstall, Cuthbert, 116, 123n, 137n

Visitation of churches, 138

Waad, Armagail, 111, 124n
Walsingham, Francis, 28, 65, 82; Cheke and Cecil, 65; family connections, 37n, 65; at Gray's Inn, 68n; at King's, 55n
Watson, Thomas, 85, 122n, 123n, 131
Wendy, Thomas, 77, 104; at Cambridge, 51n
Westminster, disputation, 122–23; effect of, 123
White, John, 122n, 123n, 131
Wilkes, Richard, 57
Willoughby, Catherine, 15, 71–72; and Bucer, 59; and Cecil, 15
Wilson, Thomas (of King's), 4, 55, 59n, 71
Wilson, Thomas (of St. John's), 54
Wolfe, Reyner, 74
Wolsey, Thomas, 43, 61
Women: educational and intellectual interests, 15, 38n, 59, 63n, 64n, 65, 68, 71, 72, 134, 135n, 144; influence, 27n; relationship to Cecil, 7, 14–15, 64–65
Wotton, Nicholas, 18n, 20, 25n, 31
Wriothesley, Thomas, 26, 62
Wrothe, Thomas, 29, 55n, 79, 82, 85, 107n; at St. John's, 54

Young, John, 84
Young, Thomas, 104